# Einstein's Rabbi

## A Tale of Science and the Soul

by

Michael M. Cohen

# SHIRES PRESS

4869 Main Street / P.O. Box 2200
Manchester Center, Vermont 05255
www.northshire.com/printondemand.php

ISBN: 978-1-60571-001-3
Library of Congress Control Number: 2008902344

Cover and interior design: Robert Turano for DeSio Associates
Princeton, NJ and New York, NY / www.desioassociates.com

Printed in the United States of America by Northshire Press
using an Espresso Book Machine from On Demand Books

This book was printed at the Northshire Bookstore, a family-owned,
independent bookstore in Manchester Center, Vermont.
We are committed to excellence in bookselling.

*Building Community, One Book at a Time*

**To My Parents**
**Alfred, z.l. and Betty Cohen**
**Who taught me the importance of music.**

Music is, to me, proof of the existence of God.

*Kurt Vonnegut*

Sing a new song to the Lord, Sing to the Eternal all the earth.

*Psalm 96*

Well, I do not think that it is necessarily the case that science and religion are natural opposites. In fact, I think that there is a very close connection between the two. Further, I think that science without religion is lame and, conversely, that religion without science is blind. Both are important and should work hand-in-hand. It seems to me that whoever doesn't wonder about the truth in religion and in science might as well be dead.

*Albert Einstein*

Day after day the word goes forth;
night after night the story is told.
Soundless the speech, voiceless the talk;
yet the story is echoed throughout the world.

*Psalm 19*

Anyhow Einstein has rendered us poor preachers a good turn by helping us put across a new idea in religion, something we could never have done ourselves.

*Rabbi Mordechai Kaplan*
*Diary, December 11, 1930*

# Table of Contents

Introduction . . . . . . . . . . . . . . . . . . . . . . . . . . . . . .iii

1. The Echo of the Universe . . . . . . . . . . . . . . . . . . . . . .1
2. Michelangelo's David . . . . . . . . . . . . . . . . . . . . . . . .2
3. Washington's Crossing of the Delaware . . . . . . . . . . . .4
4. Leningrad . . . . . . . . . . . . . . . . . . . . . . . . . . . . . .12
5. Jerusalem . . . . . . . . . . . . . . . . . . . . . . . . . . . . . .16
6. Touching the Infinite . . . . . . . . . . . . . . . . . . . . . .23
7. Kabbalah . . . . . . . . . . . . . . . . . . . . . . . . . . . . . .30
8. Corina . . . . . . . . . . . . . . . . . . . . . . . . . . . . . . .42
9. Early Changes . . . . . . . . . . . . . . . . . . . . . . . . . . .45
10. Riding on a Beam of Light . . . . . . . . . . . . . . . . . . .50
11. Billy . . . . . . . . . . . . . . . . . . . . . . . . . . . . . . . .59
12. Secrets . . . . . . . . . . . . . . . . . . . . . . . . . . . . . . .62
13. Religious Fanaticism . . . . . . . . . . . . . . . . . . . . . .72
14. Choices . . . . . . . . . . . . . . . . . . . . . . . . . . . . . . .87
15. Prague and Kafka . . . . . . . . . . . . . . . . . . . . . . . . .91
16. Berlin . . . . . . . . . . . . . . . . . . . . . . . . . . . . . . .102
17. September 11th . . . . . . . . . . . . . . . . . . . . . . . . .123
18. Zion and Cosmic Religion . . . . . . . . . . . . . . . . . .130
19. Wrestling . . . . . . . . . . . . . . . . . . . . . . . . . . . . .148
20. A Blessing . . . . . . . . . . . . . . . . . . . . . . . . . . . . .153
    Coda . . . . . . . . . . . . . . . . . . . . . . . . . . . . . . . .158
    Author's Note . . . . . . . . . . . . . . . . . . . . . . . . . .161
    About the Author . . . . . . . . . . . . . . . . . . . . . . . .161
    Permissions . . . . . . . . . . . . . . . . . . . . . . . . . . . .162

# Introduction

This novella has had a twenty-eight-year journey from the time it was first born into this world as an undergraduate paper until its present publication by Shires Press. When we gaze upon the light from a distant star, because of the time it takes for the light to reach us—light years—the star itself may actually have changed and would appear different if we could look at it in real time. Writing contains a similar process but in a different direction. The final product that we read is its "real time"; however, behind it lies many changes that connect us to its original form.

During the spring of 1980 I took a course on Albert Einstein with Dr. Henry Steffens at the University of Vermont. We were given an assignment to write a paper. I decided to focus on the question of science and religion and Einstein's relationship to Judaism (foreshadowing my entering rabbinical college three years later). I remember sitting on the floor of my Loomis Street apartment looking at different piles of research index cards divided by subject. I was at a loss as to how to weave them into a paper. I then remembered the story I had heard about Einstein's rabbi a few years earlier in Leningrad and wondered what it would be like to have a conversation with him. It was then that the conversation form of the paper, and eventually this novella, was born. I had mononucleosis at the time, so Dr. Steffens allowed me to give it to him not typed, but hand printed on yellow legal paper.

If memory serves me correctly I sent it out to a few publishers shortly after graduating from UVM that year. After a few years as the rabbi of the Israel Congregation in Manchester Center, Vermont, I returned to the work and added to the voice of the rabbi. In the fall of 2001 the novella found its way to Joanna Hill and Laura Barrett at Templeton Press, where for a while it went through some changes. While Templeton did not publish it, Joanna and Laura were extremely helpful in the novella's continued growth.

During the next year, there where many readers and rewrites of the manuscript. My parents were critical to its development during this period, as were my in-laws, Libby and Winfred Hill. Rob Turano of DeSio Associates was also very helpful. More recently he designed the cover and formatted the novella. Other readers included Jamaica Kincaid, Rev. Steve Buechner, Janet Irving, Rabbi John Schechter, Cantor Riki Lippitz, Susan Kelly, Sara and Nat Dolsky, Kathy and John Wright, Eric Barnum, Pam Gordon, Rabbi Jack Cohen, Rabbi Zalman Schacter-Shlomi, Rabbi Ira Eisenstein, z.l., as well as friends at my other home, Kibbutz Ketura: Sara Cohen, David Factor, Miriam Erez, and Bill Slott. Not only did all of these readers provide constructive comments, but, more important, their belief in this project gave me the strength to keep going with it.

In the summer of 2002 Rabbi Jonathan Kligler introduced me to Kenny Wapner of Peekamoose Productions. For the next two years Kenny put in many hours as he moved the novella from its one-conversation format to many conversations and added literary arcs and curves. I am greatly indebted to Kenny for the many improvements he brought to the manuscript. As Kenny had me do the many rewrites during that period, Hal Klopper was an invaluable part of the process and made suggestions along the way. I also called upon a number of people for factual information during that period: Dr. Daniel Matt, Dr. Larry Fine, Dr. Jon Machta, Dr. Martin Spergel,

Rav Goldenberg, Dr. Amy Jill Levine, Dr. Elizabeth Sherman, Rev. Tom Breidenthal, Joshua Rosenberg, Varsity Wines, and Eitan Segal Wines. Lee Stern, z.l., shared his collection of Einstein papers from when he knew Einstein, as did Gillett Griffin, who also made the time to meet with me. During this period my parents continued to give me feedback and other helpful readers also appeared: Deborah Harris, Rabbi Bob and Sally Freedman, Sandy Sussman, Linda and Brock Evans, and Jeremy Dworkin. Laura Brass and Jane Susswein also provided helpful suggestions.

More recently Arnold Dolin was helpful with his suggestions, as were Marc Estrin, Amos Kamil, Bill Muench, Doris Bass, Anita Grey, Jeffrey Sosnow, Susan Schick, Micah Cohen, Robin Galender, Ellen Kastel, Ina Cohen, Rabbi Susan Silverman, and Dr. Clive Lipchin. The following agents and publishers provided suggestions and comments that allowed me to continue to believe that this book was a worthwhile endeavor that needed to see the light of day: Frances Goldin, Kris Ashley, Sarah Lazin, Rebecca Friedman, Ehud Sperling, Jud Laghi, Susan Mercandetti, Bill Gladstone, Neil Gudovitz, Josh Getzler, and Thomas McCormack.

Capella is the sixth-brightest star and is forty light years away from us. That means its light that we now see has been traveling through space for forty years. To put in another way, that light left the year the Beatles founded Apple Records, the company they established to make it easier for artists to get their projects off the ground. It was an example of the Zeitgeist that Marshall McLuhan was writing about in his understanding of the technological Global Village our world was entering.

One of the latest manifestations of that ongoing process is the invention of the Espresso Book Machine (EBM), which allows books to be published on demand without the backing of a major publishing house. For years the Northshire Bookstore, under the guidance of the Morrow Family, has been the flagship of independent bookstores in the United States. In that same independent spirit the Morrows have made the Northshire Bookstore the first, and at this time, only retail location in the U.S. for such a machine that enables authors to have their books published. As Einstein opened up new ways to understand the universe that we inhabit, these machines will alter what is possible when it comes to publishing; distant stars will no longer seem so far away. I want to thank Lucy Gardner Carson, Heather Bellanca, and Marie Leahy of the Shires Press imprint of the Northshire Bookstore for walking me through this new process. It is an honor that Einstein's Rabbi is one of their first books to be published.

Over the years I have found the following locations excellent places to write in Princeton, Evanston, New York, Jerusalem, and Washington, DC: Small World Café, Kafein, Via Della Pace, French Roast, Bubby's Pie Company, Cuba Café, Café Aroma, Café Hillel, and Ruth & Sara's Place. My thanks to the staff who provided me with the perfect locations and service for the muse to be heard.

Finally, words cannot express my love and thanks to my wife Alison and children, Roi and Shirah for all of their support these many years that I have worked on this project. They are the constellation that I thank the stars I am part of.

Manchester Center, Vermont
March 14, 2008

# 1

## The Echo of the Universe

Einstein's rabbi lived for another twenty years—years filled with many more conversations. I did not know that, at that moment when his wife Eden told me that he had suffered a heart attack and had been taken to the Princeton Hospital. I thought I had lost him and, with him, my guide; the one who had touched my soul and showed me the way to the path I needed to take. When I told him my fears, he scoffed at me and quoted a letter Einstein wrote to his friend and fellow physicist Michele Besso's widow after Besso's death: "In quitting this strange world he has once again preceded me by just a little. That doesn't mean anything. For we convinced physicists the distinction between past, present, and future is only an illusion, however persistent."

Time, as Einstein discovered in his Special Theory of Relativity, is not the constant we assume it is, but is warped by the mass of the earth spinning through space. Those "unfinished" statues of Michelangelo in Florence so intrigued Einstein because they falsely captured a moment in time; as though a moment could only be now, devoid simultaneously of past and future. It is perhaps why God's name in Hebrew is the verb "to be," with its past, present, and future forms combined into one unified word. Time, according to Einstein, is a continuum that fluctuates—like stepping into the

1

moving water of a stream.

So what do we latch on to? The timeless echo of the universe; that sound that only our soul can hear, that so inspired the Book of Psalms. I had first experienced that connection standing next to my grandfather, surrounded by a magical sea of white prayer shawls as I listened to the hum of prayer that filled the air around us.

That echo provides our lives with meaning. It reminds us that our lives matter and are important. That echo can come in many forms, through many different messengers. It came to me through what my parents passed on to me, and in fighting them for what they did not convey. It came to me most through Einstein's rabbi, blessed be his memory, and through the words and life and soul of Einstein himself. It came to me in a chance meeting one night in Jerusalem—and it came to me in a dream.

# 2

# Michelangelo's David

When I first met Einstein's rabbi, the dream returned, and wouldn't go away. It had first appeared in my childhood long before I learned about the family secret. A secret that, once revealed, would shed light on the formation of my Jewish identity and spiritual quest. The secret had been well hidden, like a message in a dream, but in retrospect hints and clues appeared along the way. Like the Biblical desert that appears barren and empty at first glance, but if one pays close enough attention a story unfolds.

My parents, my brother Nathan, ten years older than me, and I were touring Europe and had gone to the Galleria dell'Accademia in Florence to view Michelangelo's David. My father was on sabbatical from his tenured job as a professor of history at Trenton State College. My mother, a college art teacher, was enraptured by Michelangelo's masterpiece.

"Look at him," she said to us. "Not since the Greeks has our culture produced anything so beautiful, so strong. He is the Platonic ideal: Man in all his perfection of form."

This was how my parents saw the world, in a secular and rational way. But something in me wanted a different David. Even at the age of nine I knew enough Bible to wonder why my mother didn't say that David had saved the Israelites from the Philistines, or was one of the Kings of Israel, or that Jewish tradition ascribed the Book of Psalms to him.

A few days later we were at the harbor in Genoa getting ready to board a ship to Israel. Docked next our boat was the Italian steamship Michelangelo. The previous week it had been hit by a tidal wave in the Atlantic Ocean. The wave had smashed through the bridge and the first-class area of the ocean liner, killing two passengers and a crew member. The front of the boat was a mess. The sight of such a huge ocean liner wounded and damaged like that made me scared to board our ship.

That night as I lay in my bunk bed, as the boat gently rocked from side to side as it made its way down the Italian coast, I dreamt the dream for the first time. I was back in the Galleria. My parents were on either side of me, holding my hands as we walked down the great hall where Michelangelo's David stood. As we approached the David, I noticed that his head had shifted slightly and his eyes were looking right at me. He raised his right arm, his fingers unfurled, and he pointed at my chest. I felt a great warmth in my heart, but I was also afraid. I started trembling as the huge statue leapt from its pedestal, lithe and filled with volition, and strode toward me, its marble feet splintering the floor. I turned to run. My parents were no longer holding my hands, and I was alone. I ran down the empty gallery and pushed open the huge wooden doors of the museum. Instead of finding myself on the Via Ricasoli, I was on the Mount of Olives in Jerusalem, looking down the Kidron Valley at King Solomon's Temple. A plume of black smoke curled from its vast courtyard. I then found myself standing in front of the altar, face to face with a goat. Blood seeped from the corners of the goat's eyes and dripped from its mouth. The goat's legs buckled as it fell to the side, and I woke up.

I dreamt the dream another two or three times that year and not again until after my first visit with Einstein's rabbi. Since then, the dream has returned with greater frequency and greater intensity. I must ask him about it next time I see him.

# 3

# Washington's Crossing of the Delaware

I grew up in Ewing, New Jersey. Its contented middle class described Ewing as a suburb of Trenton, while its more culturally inclined residents, my parents included, called Ewing a satellite of Princeton, taking advantage of its close proximity to that bastion of intellect.

The latter sounded better, but the former was more accurate. Ewing's identity was based on what it was near, not what it was. At a young age, growing up within the gravitational field of Princeton, listening to my parents talk of it with a proprietary pride undercut by longing, I intuitively knew that most of us live that way, too—in the suburbs of the great ideas of people like Einstein.

I did not, of course, understand Einstein's theories at that point, but I developed an early fascination with him on my eighth birthday when my father said, after I blew out the candles on my banana chocolate birthday cake, "Your birthday and Einstein's are both today." My mother chimed in, "Einstein lived up the road in Princeton."

My father added, "And your great-uncle Frank Schwartzstein was asked by the Governor of New Jersey to be part of the delegation of Jewish leaders in New Jersey who welcomed Einstein here."

This information greatly impressed me and sealed my early interest in the great thinker.

While at that age I did not understand Einstein's effect on history, I did know that Ewing had had its own moment in history. After George Washington crossed the Delaware, he had to march across what would become Ewing to get to Trenton. His march took him a few hundred yards from our house.

When I was a few years older, Nathan and I would often retrace that march biking from our house to Washington Crossing Historic Park. Though he was a decade older, he always made time for me, even as the distractions of high school life increased for him. By eleventh grade he was taller than both my parents and was one of the stars of the Ewing High swimming team. For the longest time I could not understand why my parents had waited so long to have me.

We would pack a lunch and end up on the Pennsylvania side of the Delaware River. After lunch, which always included our mother's prized brownies, we would go see Emanuel Gottlieb Leutze's famous painting, George Washington Crossing the Delaware, which for many years was housed there in a small building before it was eventually moved to the Metropolitan Museum of Art in New York City. When we would get back home our parents always asked us if we had strained our eyes enough while looking at the painting to make out the shoreline of Ewing in the background.

Then our father, an expert on all things Ewing, would say, "That painting has numerous historical inaccuracies in it."

"Yes, Papa, we know. You said that last time."

As the years rolled on we were able to recite all the mistakes to our parents, which gave them great pleasure. Nathan would start: "First, the crossing took place in the middle of the night, not at daybreak. Second, Washington never would have stood in such a boat, and the boats in the painting are not the kind that Washington used. In addition, the thirteen-starred flag had yet to be even conceived." One day after we came back from a ride our father said to me, "The other day you asked me to explain Einstein's Theory of Relativity. That painting is Relativity in a nutshell. It is a perfect example of how we accept what we experience, what we see, as the truth. And that is just what Albert Einstein challenged. In his 1905 Special Theory of Relativity he took Newton's understanding that time and space are absolute and stood it on its head by showing that measurements of time and distance deviate, since everything is constantly moving relative to everything else. In short he showed that Newton was limited, and if Newton's understanding was limited then how we understood the universe was limited too."

My knowledge of Newton at that time consisted of gravity and an apple falling from a tree. I wondered if there was something wrong with gravity. So I took an apple from the refrigerator and went outside and stood on the front porch of our house. I turned to make sure no one was watching, and let the apple go. It dropped to the ground. Gravity was still working. I was relieved.

When I was twelve, my parents and I went to see the Martha Graham Dance Company at McCarter Theatre on the Princeton campus. When we passed Einstein's house on Mercer Street my father said, "That's where Einstein lived!" I strained my head around in the back seat to keep the house in sight for as long as possible. "Perhaps you'll grow up and become a great scientist like Einstein," my mother added.

The program notes that night had a wonderful anecdote about Graham and Helen Keller. Once Helen Keller visited the dance studio where Graham's dancers were rehearsing. To let her get a better sense of what dance was all about, Graham had Keller put her hands around a dancer's waist and then had him leap straight up off the wooden dance floor. Keller beamed. "That's just like having an idea!" she said.

After I read this, I would always think of it as we passed Einstein's house. The image of an idea as a leap into the air, a leap into the unknown, an escape from gravity and that which holds us down, seemed all the more significant when I thought of Einstein making those vast leaps beyond what was known and accepted. I wondered what it would be like to take such a leap.

My father, aware of my growing interest in Einstein, dropped a bomb at the dinner table one night, announcing that Einstein had been cremated around the corner from our house on Lower Ferry Road.

"But wasn't he Jewish?" I asked. I knew that cremation was against Jewish law.

"Yes, but he was a secular Jew, like us," my father answered.

"And Joseph, you must understand that following Jewish law is not what makes one a Jew. It's about being a good person. That's what the mitzvot are."

Einstein a secular Jew? I hoped that somehow Einstein's relationship to Judaism was more complicated than that. My father's answer left me dissatisfied for another reason, too. I knew from my maternal grandfather, Zayda, as I called him, that a mitzvah was a commandment, not just a good deed, and that there were 613 of them.

For the Rabbis of the Talmud, Kabbalah, and Jewish philosophy, the letters of the Torah are the DNA of the Universe, and like DNA, they contain information that is hidden and complex. One tool in decoding them is gematria, whereby each letter is given a numerical value. For example soolam, which means "ladder," adds up to 130, as does "Sinai." From this a connection is made between the dream of Jacob's ladder and the Revelation at Mount Sinai. Another gematria is the word garti, which means "I lived" and whose numerical value is 613, the same number of the mitzvot or commandments in the Torah, thus teaching us we should live our lives filled with mitzvot. I felt that we were living only a fraction of our tradition.

Despite my grandfather's definition of a mitzvah, we lived our lives like most American Jews-not with a sense of being commanded by God, but, rather, choosing from the Tradition passed on to us those commandments we liked and found convenient, while discarding or ignoring the others.

I wondered: Is that what Einstein did?

My parents, like so many of their generation, were products of the melting pot of America. Between 1890 and 1920, the United States took in 18 million immigrants; many of them Poles, Irish, Germans, Austrians, Swedes, Slavs, Italians, and Jews. The term "melting pot," coined in 1908 by an English Jew, Israel Zangwill, was the title of his play, which explored the transforming effect on immigrants to America. All groups faced similar choices about what to retain or discard from the way they had lived their lives before coming to America. Many Jews chose to dispense with the customs and practices of Judaism. Off came the yarmulkes. The kosher kitchen disappeared, along with the lighting of candles on Friday night. These Jews became part of mainstream America, and they raised their children to become part of it as well.

Along with this assimilation and integration into American life there was a rise in American anti-Semitism. By the 1930s, for example, U.S. Patent Number 2,026,077 was the "kike killer," a hardwood truncheon. The following decade saw the Second World War and the Holocaust, the Shoah, along with the birth of the modern State of Israel. All of these raised serious and complex theological questions for the generation that came of age during those two decades. Too often those questions were dismissed by rabbis through simplistic theological answers, or a myopic hysteria about the survival of the Jewish people, creating a paralysis that prevented many of them from taking the necessary steps to make Judaism more relevant and meaningful to their lives.

My parents considered themselves to be cultural Jews: they understood that Judaism had meaningful values, even if they did not believe that the source of those values was divine. They felt part of the Jewish people—a shared history that also included a culture of poetry, music, and food. They had a sense of belonging to a tribe with shared experiences and a common concern for the Jewish future.

I had a classic American Jewish upbringing. We celebrated Rosh Hashanah, Yom Kippur, Hanukah, a little Purim, and Passover. No Shabbat, no Sukkot, no Kosher home, and no weekly attendance at synagogue. This, I would later find out, was not much different from the kind of house in which Einstein grew up. I would learn from Einstein's rabbi that his name should have been Abraham, for his grandfather, but since his parents found the name too Jewish they kept the first letter, as was a common practice among the more assimilated Jews, and named him Albert instead.

I felt a vague frustration and disappointment with my family's approach to Judaism, especially when I went to visit my maternal grandparents, who belonged to an Orthodox synagogue in Perth Amboy, New Jersey. While they had assimilated, they had kept a healthy remnant of religious observance in their lives. I loved going to services at the old synagogue when we visited them on Shabbat or a holiday.

When my grandfather put on his talis, his prayer shawl, he would cover me with it, bend over, and recite the blessing for wrapping oneself in a talis. "Zayda," I would say to him. "This is just like being in a tent. Let's stay here awhile." We would huddle together, smiling at each other, until my Uncle Alec would nudge my grandfather and whisper, "Services are about to begin." Then my grandfather would lift the talis from us and drape it over his shoulders.

The service would start with a chant, an invocation, a great wave rolling over me in an ancient tongue, a language that seemed filled with desert, wind, and stone. I would look up and feel as though I was in a magical forest of tall white trees as the men around us swayed and rocked back and forth during their prayers. There was an ineffable feeling of belonging, comfort, and safety that I experienced sitting next to my grandfather, near the front of the synagogue, surrounded by a sea of white prayer shawls.

My grandfather knew of my interest in Einstein. One day, when we were still under his talis, he said: "You know, Einstein once remarked, 'I want to know God's thoughts. The rest are details.'"

Those words struck a chord within me and I wanted to

know more. "Does that mean he believed in God, Zayda?"

"My good friend Zeigfried Schweitzer told me he once asked Einstein if he believed in God."

I was barely able to contain myself. "What was his answer?"

My grandfather smiled. "Einstein replied: 'I bow before the Unknown.' Einstein was a mystic scientist or, as some would say, a mystic who was a scientist."

"But Zayda, how could such a great scientist be a mystic?"

"Why are you so sure that science and mysticism can't go together?"

Services continued. We heard the chazzan, the cantor, chanting hacol yodoocha, "God who daily opens the gates of the heavens, the casements of the eastern sky, bringing forth the sun from its dwelling place, the moon from its abode, illuminating the whole world ..."

My grandfather kissed me on the forehead and lifted the talis from us, draping it with practiced elegance across his shoulders. The murmuring of the congregation followed the cantor's melodious words. The prayers were laden with fragrance, ineffably sweet yet sharp, too. I breathed them in as they rustled around me like the wind at dawn.

When I stayed with Zayda, we would say the Sh'ma together right before he put me to bed. I slept in a single bed with a wooden backboard with little beads inlaid on its edge. I slept under a quilt that had a white-on-white design. The bedroom was at the end of a long hall that looked out over a small backyard. I felt completely secure there, even though I was away from everyone, down at the end of that long dim hall.

"Sh'ma Yisrael, Hear, O Israel, the Lord is our God, the Lord is one," my grandfather and I chanted together.

One night after we had recited the Sh'ma and soon after our

conversation in Shul about Einstein the mystic scientist, my grandfather said, "Do you know, Joseph, why these words of all the words in the Torah are the most important? Why we are commanded as Jews to say them twice a day?"

"That's easy, Zayda. Because they talk about there being only one God in the world."

"You're right, but it's deeper than that. We have a Yiddish expression: Alles ist Got. All is God. A unity connects everything and everybody in the universe. That's why we say the Sh'ma; to remind us of this."

# 4

# Leningrad

A few summers later, my family took a trip to Eastern Europe and the Soviet Union. We traveled to Moscow, Kiev, Odessa, and, finally, north to St. Petersburg, then called Leningrad. The main purpose of our trip was to meet relatives, most of whom wanted to escape the oppression of Soviet anti-Semitism and Communism and emigrate to Israel or the United States.

We spent the summer, visiting museums, castles, cathedrals, and other historic and cultural sights. While my parents were not very religious, in all our travels they also had us find the synagogue wherever we were, even though they had no intention of going to services. This was a Jewish intermarriage: my father an agnostic and my mother an atheist. Discovering the synagogues sent a clear message to me that my Jewish identity was important and mattered.

We ventured forth in the pouring rain immediately after checking into our hotel. Our Intourist bus dropped us off in front of the synagogue's worn wooden doors, where we were met by the shames, or caretaker—an old man in a frayed suit jacket.

The synagogue was built in a Moorish style that I had learned to recognize both from the style of my grandparents' synagogue in Perth Amboy, and from the many we had already visited on our trip. Its walls were painted yellow and white, its ceiling patterned in stucco arches. It smelled of dust, old wood, damp stone, and onions. Unlike most of the synagogues of Eastern Europe, it had been spared the ravages of the Nazis. It didn't feel as though it was much used for worship; and, as with so many synagogues we had visited, I felt as though we had entered a relic, an empty shell from a different age.

The shames welcomed us. He shuffled forward, smelling of tobacco, beckoning to us with his hand, smiling with broken teeth that were the color of tea. He wore slippers and his tzitzit limply flapped as he moved down the aisles, his back bent, and his hands at his sides. We followed him to the front of the big domed main room. He showed us where the Torah scroll stood behind the battered doors of the Ark and gave us little bits of history. In 1868 Tsar Alexander II granted Jews the right to live in St. Petersburg, and in the 1890s, when 15,000 Jews lived in the city, the synagogue was built.

The shames spoke in Yiddish. My father, who had been raised in a Yiddish-speaking home, translated. The shames seated us in a small bare room, insisting we drink L'chaim, "to life," as was the custom. He said he wanted to tell us a story. I could hardly believe it when the story turned out to be about Einstein!

"Most people are surprised by this story," the shames said, each word perfumed by the sweet, acrid odor of schnapps. "It takes place in the days of Stalin, may his name be forever forgotten. A group of scientists were allowed to visit the United States. They traveled through your country, visiting many other scientists. At the end of their stay, they went to Princeton to visit Dr. Albert Einstein. I heard this story from one of the scientists who was Jewish and stopped by here soon after their visit.

"The scientists were greeted at the door by Einstein's stepdaughter, Margot, who showed them into the living room. Einstein was busy with another guest. While they waited, Helen Dukas, Einstein's energetic secretary and housekeeper, was sent upstairs to get three books. The scientists were stunned when she returned, carrying the Five Books of Moses, the Book of Psalms, and the Book of Job.

"One scientist turned to the others and asked, 'What could he want those books for?' Another asked, 'Who could he be speaking to?'

"Some time passed, and finally Dr. Einstein and his guest emerged. The guest had a short beard and looked much younger than Dr. Einstein. As his host showed him to the door, the scientists noticed that the guest wore a yarmulke. I must tell you that these were proud secular Soviet scientists and the sight of this yarmulke left them speechless. Not only that, but Einstein and his guest were laughing about a supper party they had been to the previous evening. A professor of history had asked Dr. Einstein whom from history he would most like to meet. He had expected the answer to be someone like Newton or Archimedes, but he was stunned when Dr. Einstein said, 'Moses,' adding, 'I would like to ask him if he ever thought that his people would obey his law so long!'

"When Dr. Einstein greeted his Soviet guests, one of the

scientists could not help asking, 'Who was that man?'

"Einstein replied, 'Oh, he is my rabbi.'

"'Why would a great scientist like you need a rabbi?'

"Dr. Einstein replied with a twinkle in his eyes, 'Whenever I have a problem I cannot solve, I speak with my rabbi.'"

"Who would have thought," said my father as we were leaving, "that Einstein would have consulted with a rabbi? I know enough about him to know that he believed in rational scientific laws, not all that nonsense of the Bible!"

I held my tongue, but I knew that another piece of my Einstein puzzle had fallen into place. Einstein's Jewish identity must have been more complex than my parents had acknowledged. I wondered how he had managed to bridge the gap between science and religion. My upbringing told me that they occupied polar extremes: science was rational; religion, mystical. Science was based on hard fact; religion on faith. Science was logical; religion, superstitious. Science asked how; religion, why. Looking back I see how I felt cornered by those opposites. Dualities. Something deep inside me already sensed that these dualities were false.

Shortly after we returned from the Soviet Union, my grandfather died. Something in my inclination toward Judaism died with him, or, more precisely, became moribund. Perhaps anticipating this, he left money in his will specifically for me to travel to Israel.

# 5

# Jerusalem

In Jerusalem worlds overlap and interconnect like the gears of a clock. In Jerusalem, both the dream and the reality of Jewish history weave the backdrop for personal histories and stories. All is connected, the personal as well as the national tale. One summer my story became one of those tales.

It was summer. All summers, all seasons, have their own flavor, their own sounds, and their own identity. That summer was no different. It was the summer that America celebrated its Bicentennial. It was the summer of Jimmy Carter and Gerald Ford. It was the summer George Brett played baseball the way it was supposed to be played. It was the summer to be in America—particularly if you had just graduated or, as I felt, had just been "liberated" from the "prison" of high school. Instead, I would spend that summer in Israel, using the money my grandfather had left me. He had also left me with our conversation about Einstein, the mystic scientist. But since his death there was no one to talk to about it. My parents only wanted to hear about Einstein the scientist, and the local rabbi thought it was no more than a cute notion.

Through an aunt, I had found out that I could take part in archeological excavations on the southern slopes of the ancient Temple Mount in Jerusalem. When my parents saw me off, they cautioned: "Now don't come back religious!" referring to the phenomenon known as ba'al tsuvah, when secular Jews become observant, often after a trip to Israel. Did they sense, even then, that I was looking for something different from the way they had lived their lives as Jews?

I arrived in Jerusalem during a time of relative tranquility. Those were the good days when Jews and Arabs were getting to know each other doing business together. The complexities and contradiction of occupation, no matter how benign at first, had yet to materialize. Those of the generation that would lead the first Intifada were only babies and small children. Secular Jews filled the crowded and colorful alleys of the Shook, or Arab market, on Shabbat. That was the summer when I would discover the sights, smells, sounds, and people of the Old City's four quarters—Christian, Muslim, Jewish, and Armenian. There was something else I would discover that summer as well.

The group stayed at the hostel of the Jerusalem YMCA, pronounced IMKA in Hebrew. Standing across the street from the King David Hotel, its rounded Moorish style bell tower is one of the most recognizable features of the Jerusalem skyline. Built in 1933, it was designed by Q. L. Harmon, the man who also designed the Empire State Building. Its three architectural sections were meant to represent the aims of the YMCA—the development of the body, mind, and spirit—as well as the three monotheistic faiths that had all been born in the Middle East. In 1947 the United Nations' Special Committee on Palestine held its Jerusalem sessions there, leading to the Partition Plan of that year.

Up at 5:00 a.m. and out by 5:30 a.m., we would walk in the still, cool, dry, morning air scented by sweet Jasmine bushes. Past the King David Hotel, down into the Hinnom Valley, through the Mammilla district, which still bore scars from the Six Day War and the nineteen years from 1948 until 1967, when Jerusalem had been divided between Israel and Jordan. Then up the slope and through the Jaffa Gate and into the Old City. The Jaffa Gate was one of the Old City's eight gates that had been built by Suleiman the Magnificent in the sixteenth century. In Arabic it was known as Bab el Khalil, Gate of the Friend, referring to Abraham, the Friend of God. Once inside the gate, we were in the Christian Quarter, then a quick turn to the right and we were in the Armenian Quarter. From there we entered the Jewish Quarter, which at the time was undergoing extensive excavations, revealing its ancient Jewish past.

I had first visited Jerusalem in the spring of 1967, the year the dream started, when I was nine years old. That year my father was an exchange professor from what was then called Trenton State College, to the University of Frankfurt. Twenty years after the Second World War I learned about some of the dynamics of Germany that had forced Einstein to leave during the Nazi era.

My teacher in the Westend Schule, Herr Seigel, had fought in General Erwin Rommel's elite Africa Korps. He was captured in May 1943 with the collapse of Rommel's forces and was sent to Camp Atterbury, Indiana, where he was a prisoner of war for the remainder of the war. I was born in Bloomington, Indiana, while my father was completing his doctorate in history at Indiana University. Rommel meant nothing to me in third grade, but to Seigel someone from Indiana was like a long-lost relative, and so this young Jewish Hoosier and a former member of Rommel's army formed an instant bond. I had another advocate in the principal of the school, Rector Weld, who had fought in the German underground against Hitler.

One of the more bizarre moments of that year occurred when we were looking for an apartment and the landlady we spoke with started ranting about all the apartments she had lost during the war due to the Allied bombing. As we left I remember my mother saying to my father, "It's a good thing she didn't know that we are Jewish." To which my fathered replied, "I think she did, and that's why she had that fit in there. In her own way she was able to blame the Jews again."

In Jerusalem, on that first visit, we were not allowed into the Old City to visit the holy Jewish sights there. At that time, Jews were not permitted to cross over into East Jerusalem, as it was in the hands of the Jordanians. The closest Jews could approach the Old City was Mount Zion, where we could look over the ancient walls of the Old City and try to get a glimpse of what was on the other side. On the horizon and above the Old City walls Mount Scopus housed the original Hebrew University of Jerusalem. Opened in 1923, Einstein had given the inaugural address there. In 1967 it was an empty island separated from Israeli West Jerusalem, according to the terms of the 1948 Armistice Agreement. A few months later it would be reunited with West Jerusalem on the last day of fighting during the Six Day War.

A fence separated Mount Zion from the Jordanian side. While we were there, a young Arab shepherdess was tending her goats on the other side of the fence. The clanging from the little bells the goats wore around their necks filled the air. Something deep inside of me knew that I was supposed to be on the other side as well. I stuck my arm through the metal fence, plucked a blade of grass, and brought it to our side.

Nine years later, the fence was gone, Jerusalem was united, and I was within the Old City Walls.

On that first morning of the dig, the leader of our group, a rabbi from New Jersey, said, "Before we go to the dig, we are going to make a short stop at the holiest spot we Jews have—the Western Wall."

Suddenly, we were standing before the Wall in the plaza

that had been created after the unification of the city for the large numbers of people who gathered there on Shabbat and other Jewish holidays. There it stood, a remnant of the colossal wall Herod the Great had built almost two thousand years earlier to support the Temple platform. Since the Temple's destruction in the year 70 C.E. it had been the focus of Jewish pilgrims coming to Zion.

Now I stood there. In the large plaza that faced the Wall, I sensed a low-level voltage in the air: a permanent buzz of prayers and conversations. Around me, some in the group began to cry, others approached the Wall and kissed it, and others, as was the custom, wrote notes and placed them in the crevices between the massive limestone stones. The Wall above ground consists of twenty-four rows of stones reaching a height of more than sixty feet. However, this was somewhat deceiving. There are another nineteen rows hidden underground, reaching all the way to the natural rock of the Tyropoeon Valley, which was the ground level when Herod rebuilt the Temple around the year 20 C.E. Today when people approach the Wall to pray, they are actually standing, hovering, almost sixty feet above where Jewish pilgrims and Roman occupying soldiers stood when the retaining walls were originally built.

Many of the stones measure three feet in height and ten feet in width, with some as long as forty feet and weighing over one hundred tons. To make the Wall stable enough to carry the immense weight, each row of stones was set back a few centimeters from the row below it. Because of this, the Wall actually slants out slightly at the bottom toward the worshipers.

What did I do? I stood there and felt nothing. Fear came over me. Why don't I feel anything? I asked myself. There must be something wrong with me. Searching for reassurance, I heard my parents inside me saying, "But it's only a wall of stones."

We left for the dig. The lingering question of the Wall was

quickly replaced by the excitement of excavating a site where the Roman Tenth Legion had quartered almost two thousand years earlier. I loved the work. It was in the open air, it was physical, and there was always the possibility with each shovelful of dirt making a discovery.

Each day, we would pass the Wall on our way to and from the dig. And each time I passed it, I hoped that something would wake in my heart. I would have settled for a vague feeling of affinity or kinship, let alone a deep sense of connection or awe. But nothing happened. So it continued throughout the summer. My thoughts began to turn to college and a new phase of my life. Still, there was the Wall.

One night during the last week of the dig, I lay in bed, unable to sleep. I snuck past the night guard of the hostel and made my way through the dark stillness of the Shook to the Wall. Floodlights illuminated its chiseled contours. A black sky rose behind it. The night was cool, the wind sweeping past the Mount of Olives, where Jews had been buried for thousands of years, hoping to be the first to be resurrected when the Messiah would appear. The only others there in the middle of the night in front of the Wall were a group of Bratslav Hassidim in black hats and long black coats who sang and danced in a circle, their arms on each other's shoulders. I sat down and watched them and listened to the joy in their voices. Occasionally, one of them broke ranks and did an ecstatic jig, throwing his arms in the air, rapturously clapping. I wondered what it would be like to be able to tap into such joy so consistently. The Hassidim eventually dispersed, leaving me alone with the Wall and my thoughts.

Footsteps echoed in the stone plaza. A soldier approached the Wall, a gun slung over his shoulder, and began to pray. Then I noticed there was a pregnant woman at the Wall. I could tell from her clothes that she was not religious. I stayed in the plaza for the better part of the night, watching not the Wall but the people who came there. They were young and old, men and women, religious and secular, tourists and Israelis. All had been drawn to that sacred spot.

As I was getting up to leave, one of the Hassidim, a man in his mid-twenties who had returned to the Wall, came over to me. "I noticed you when we were dancing. You haven't gone up to the Kotel the whole time you've been here. How can you leave?"

"I've been asking myself that question. But I haven't found the answer yet."

"In the book of Psalms we read, 'The earth belongs to the Lord and all it contains; the world and all its inhabitants.' We also read, 'The heavens are the heavens of God, and the earth God gave to humanity.'"

"But that doesn't make sense," I said. "According to what you said in the first sentence, God is found throughout the world, while in the second sentence God is limited to heaven, while the world is for humanity."

The Hassid smiled at me. "And how is that contradiction resolved?"

"I don't know."

"There is no contradiction. The first verse refers to before a berachah, a blessing, is said when everything in the world belongs to God, while the second verse refers to the state of things after a berachah has been said. We are able to partake and enjoy from this world only after having thanked and acknowledged God's owner-ship. Our task as humans is to elevate the holy sparks of the world, those sparks that lie dormant until we acknowledge them. Every action of ours has the potential to release those holy sparks and uncover the presence of God in this world. God needs us as much as we need God."

And then it finally struck me, what had been bothering, stopping, me from approaching the Wall. It's not the Wall, I thought. Those stones are not holy in themselves. It's the people who come here that make them holy. That insight opened something in my soul, although I barely knew what it was or where it would lead me. What I did know was that I suddenly yearned to add to and ensure the holiness of that spot, as generations had done for thousand of years before me.

Slowly, I approached the Wall. I placed my palms on its cool stones, feeling the texture of the small grooves that had been chiseled two thousand years ago. I felt both energized and confused. I wanted to kiss the Wall, but something stopped me. What would my parents think? I realized at that moment that I had to resolve the many questions of my Jewish heritage and identity. "I must find Einstein's rabbi," I said to myself, content, for the moment, to lean forward and whisper the words into the rough face of the cool stone.

# 6

# Touching the Infinite

When I returned to New Jersey from Israel, preparations for beginning my studies at the University of Vermont distracted me from the resolution I had made. However, one day while walking through the UVM campus, I wandered into the Physics Department and began a conversation with one of the professors. He said that the question of the physicist was the same as that of the philosopher: How does the world operate and how did it get started? He told me that in many ways, the Physics Department really belonged in the School of Humanities rather than the School of Sciences.

I was stunned. Here was a scientist who did not accept the disjunction of science and religion. If he felt that way, why should I not listen to what my heart had been telling me? That was the problem. Like society I had compartmentalized my life. There was my heart and there was my head, and the two were not to meet. For example, I had blocked off the week into time for classes, time studying for classes, and time for play. An hour here, three hours there, two hours here, every waking hour scheduled. "Let's face it," I thought, "it worked." My method was a way to manage life and get things done.

I walked back to my dorm room. It was time to study. But I could not shake the conversation I had just had with the physicist. As I neared the Living/Learning Center where I lived, I could see the campus's Patrick Gymnasium. That summer before I arrived the U.S. Olympic Team had held its tryouts for the U.S. Boxing team there in preparation for the 1976 Olympics, held just across the border in Montreal. Sugar Ray Leonard, along with Michael and Leon Spinks, all got their start at that gym. I must have been thinking about that when, suddenly, the Olympic flag came into my mind.

Five colored circles overlapping and interlinked. Each circle representing the five continents of the world—Europe, Africa, Asia, Australia, and the Americas. Some of the continents touch each other, but they certainly don't overlap as they do on the flag. Yet that was the point of the flag: It represents the athletes, people, cultures, and ideas of the five continents coming together. Not becoming one, not losing their identities, yet being enhanced by the encounter. That was it: Religion and Science were different, but they could also enhance each other.

I thought to myself, "I wish I could speak to Einstein about all of this now." And then I thought, "But what about his rabbi?" I decided that when I went home for Presidents' Weekend the following week, I would finally try to find Einstein's rabbi. When I came home from school I mustered my courage and called Helen Dukas, Einstein's secretary, who still lived at 112 Mercer Street and was listed in the phone book.

Dukas was quite helpful and told me where I could contact the rabbi. I called him at his Princeton home and was invited to Shabbas lunch on Saturday.

I was nervous as I walked down the one-block street to the rabbi's house on Pine Street. I had been dabbling with my Jewish identity for years. That's what I felt like—a dabbler. Well, not in everything. I excelled in high school, having been elected President of the Student Council, and I had founded the first recycling center in Ewing, for which I received a civics award from the town. And though I was only in my second semester I had been invited to take an upper-level political science class with Professor Harry Arkberg. But with my Jewish learning there was only stagnation without any level of proficiency. What did I expect from this rabbi? Could he really help me bridge the gap between who I was and who I felt I should be? I thought of scrapping the whole idea and eating a hoagie at Hoagie Haven, which I had just passed.

A large porch wrapped around the front and side of the rabbi's white clapboard house. The rabbi was sitting on the porch taking advantage of an early winter thaw, a white wool shawl draped over his shoulders. The wooden floor creaked as he gently rocked back and forth in his rocking chair. He was a small man, about seventy years old, with short white hair and a trimmed goatee. He wore a beige cardigan and a crimson silk cravat. He greeted me with a smile. It dawned on me that this was the first time I would actually converse with a rabbi. My earlier contacts with rabbis had been glancing. I hadn't even, I painfully recalled, had a Bar Mitzvah celebration, my mother being opposed to such "meaningless ritual" and my grandfather outraged but unable to overrule her. I had felt cheated and angry, and even discussed with my grandfather having a Bar Mitzvah ceremony and not telling my parents. But in the end he thought that it would cause too much upheaval, so we did not do it.

A spasm of pain crossed the rabbi's face as he reached out to shake my hand, and his knees buckled. I grabbed his arm, but he waved me off.

"They tell me I have a weak heart," he said. "But not to worry," he added when he saw my concern. "Every morning I thank God for giving me another day—another day to appreciate life and to try to improve myself!"

I noticed a book by his side. "What are you reading?" I asked.

"The Book of Psalms. This copy I actually gave to Einstein to help him with his problems. He would stop by and see me after he picked up his Nation and New Republic at Dolsky's. After he died, Miss Dukas returned it to me as a keepsake."

"What kind of problems did he come to you with?"

The rabbi shrugged, "Problems."

"Scientific problems? Religious problems?"

The rabbi pounced: "So you think there's a difference between the two!"

"Isn't there?"

"Well maybe there is and maybe there isn't. But there certainly was not a great difference for Albert."

"How do you mean?"

"Before I answer, come. Let's sit and eat."

We slowly entered the house, he in front, I behind. The rabbi called out, "Our guest has arrived. Eden, my wife," he said, pride and pleasure in his voice.

"Joseph," said Eden simply, descending the stairs. She was slightly larger than he. Her hair, thick and black with vivid streaks of gray, was pulled back and fastened with a clip, accentuating the strong lines of her handsome face. Her eyes were very blue. A double string of pearls hung over her simple green dress. As she crossed the room, I saw that she walked with a limp. I later learned she was that one in a million who had contracted polio from the vaccine when it first came out. She carried the limp with a certain grace.

"Asher has been looking forward to talking with you," she said. "He has been surprised over the years how few people have shown an interest in the spiritual side of Einstein's work. Our friend Rabbi Armond Cohen loved to tell us about the time he heard Albert tell a group of rabbis who had invited him to come and speak to them. As Albert got up to speak he said to them, 'I look up at the sky and see the stars and I see the sun going around and around and around. And I wonder, 'Who's doing all that spinning?'"

The three of us entered the dining room, awash in the light coming in through large bay windows. The rabbi chanted the blessing over the sweet red wine, his eyes closed in deep concentration, his hands holding the silver Kiddush cup. We all drank, and then the rabbi invited me to ritually wash my hands before the blessing over the bread.

He had asked if I would make the blessing, the motzi. I was petrified at the thought of saying a blessing in front of a rabbi and his wife, but I also wanted to be a gracious guest, so I agreed. Somehow, I was able to say the single sentence without making a mistake.

We started the meal with some of Eden's delicious vegetarian chopped liver. Having just participated in one of the most basic of those rituals, I asked, "Did Einstein practice Jewish ritual?"

"One day," answered the rabbi, "Albert came to see me. I had just finished my morning prayers, and I was still taking off my tefilin. He was playing with one of those small hand-held mazes, where you try to get a small metal ball into the center chamber. How he loved playing with it. Albert looked at my tefilin and just shook his head. He couldn't understand how someone like me, who he believed was worldly, could literally tie himself to a ritual. For Albert there was a vast difference between a religious approach or feeling about life, and religious practice."

"Do you mean that practice is not as important as feeling or intent?"

The rabbi sat up a bit straighter and studied me. One corner of Eden's mouth curled upward—a small secret smile that was not without irony.

"Not at all," the rabbi replied. "A feeling, an outlook, cannot be measured, but one can measure religious practice: Did you say blessings, study Torah, and give money to charity today? There is a framework with practice; an expression, an incarnation of feeling. But people can become blinded by their physical actions and forget that those actions are there to act as a spiritual springboard for one's life. Those physical actions are the means, not the ends."

This was a very important point that the rabbi made; a point that I would soon forget, with consequences that I could not completely undo.

The rabbi continued, "But Albert had no patience for such rituals, both because he saw how they could backfire, and because he felt they offered him nothing. He once said to me, 'The word God is for me nothing more than the expression and product of human weaknesses, the Bible a collection of honorable, but still primitive legends which are nevertheless pretty childish. No interpretation no matter how subtle can change this. For me the Jewish religion like all other religions is an incarnation of the most childish superstitions.' Did I try to show him otherwise? Of course I did. When it came to the philosophy of science and the theology of Judaism I would argue that the gap was not as great as this statement of his would seem to indicate. However when it came to ritual it was a lost cause," the rabbi said, shaking his head.

I had to keep myself from smiling. "You never made any headway?"

"Who's to say? One can always hope! He might not have admitted if my ideas influenced him. Remember, I was much younger than Albert, in my mid-twenties, only a year out of rabbinical college when he arrived in Princeton. He was in his mid-fifties and had already changed how we understood the universe! What had I done? At times, when it suited him, he made me aware of my deficit not only in brainpower, but also in years. Still, I think he expected me to try to make him more observant. He would have been disappointed if I had given up on him. He liked all the back and forth."

"How did you try to interest him in practice?" I asked.

"I remember one of my attempts in particular," the rabbi said. "A year before he died, Einstein gave, as he did from time to time, the opening address at the Princeton United Jewish Appeal Fund Drive banquet. Support of Israel, he said, was a sacrifice for the Jewish people that would make us stronger and enable us to strengthen those aspects of the Jewish tradition that would benefit all humanity. I was sitting next to him at the Princeton Inn, and, before I drank a glass of water, I turned to him. 'Albert,' I said, 'let me try to explain this to you again. When you drink a glass of water, it quenches your thirst. When I drink a glass of water, saying a bracha, a blessing, it transforms the moment and the action into something bigger. The blessing for a glass of water is, 'Baruch atah adonay eloheynu melech ha'olam shehakol nihyeh bidvaro: Blessed are You, Lord, our God, sovereign of the universe, Who created everything by speech.' That is to say, when I drink a glass of water I see it as a continuation of the ongoing process of Creation itself, when God created the world through speech. The blessing transforms an everyday act into something larger that touches Creation and the Infinite. Just think: there is no new water. It's all recycled from the beginning of Creation.' Albert just looked at me, raised his bushy eyebrows, and then started to scribble a mathematical formula on a piece of paper. He said not a word, but it reminded me that he touched the Infinite using finite methods every day as well."

We both sat silently for a minute absorbing this thought. I let my breath out in a long sigh.

"Yes," said the rabbi. "There are many ways to touch God."

When he said that, a feeling of relief washed through me.

# 7

# Kabbalah

Eden brought a noodle casserole to the table and served me. The rabbi then returned to the thread of our conversation. "I want to get back to your original questions about the difference between science and religion. Einstein was often asked about his views on this topic.

Let me quote from a letter he once wrote to me." The rabbi rose and went across the hall to his study. Through the open study door, I saw that he had a photograph of Michelangelo's David on one of the walls, which probably explains why I dreamt my David dream that night, for the first time in many years.

The rabbi returned with two overstuffed folders, papers of all sizes sticking out from their sides. "'You will hardly find one among the profounder sort of scientific minds without a particular religious feeling of his own,'" the rabbi read. "'That religious feeling takes the form of a rapturous amazement at the harmony of natural law, which reveals an intelligence of such superiority that, compared with it, all systematic thinking and acting of human beings is an utterly insignificant reflection. This feeling is the guiding principle of his life and work, in so far as he succeeds in keeping himself from the shackles of selfish desire. It is beyond question closely akin to that which has possessed the religious geniuses of all ages.'"

He paused, put the letter down and looked up at me. "I haven't read that in a while," he said. "It is good to read it again. It is very similar to the idea of my good friend Rabbi Abraham Heschel, of blessed memory, who taught the concept of 'radical amazement.' Heschel lived his life with constant awareness of the mystical.

"But, Joseph—and this is very important—Heschel also worked to redeem the world and make it a better place. He championed civil rights causes. After marching with Dr. King, he said: 'For many of us the march from Selma to Montgomery was both protest and prayer. Legs are not lips, and walking is not kneeling. And yet our legs uttered songs. Even without words, our march was worship. I felt my legs were praying.'

"Heschel said that as children we respond to the world with awe and wonder. Too often, as we get older, we lose those feelings. Our imagination dims. Einstein's imagination, I believe, never did.

"His colleague, Leopold Infeld, once said to me, 'The greatness of Einstein lies in his tremendous imagination, in the unbelievable obstinacy with which he pursues his problems. Originality is the most essential factor in important scientific work ... I often had this picture in mind while watching Einstein work. There is a most vital mechanism that constantly turns his brain. It is the sublimated vital force. Sometimes it is even painful to watch. Einstein may speak about politics, listen kindly to requests and answer questions properly, but one feels behind this external activity the calm, watchful contemplation of scientific problems, that the mechanism of his brain works without interruption. It is a constant motion that nothing can stop. Other scientists have a switch that allows them to turn off or at least to decelerate the mechanism by a detective story, exciting parties, sex or a movie. There is no such switch in Einstein's brain. The mechanism is never turned off.'"

"Do you think that was true?"

The rabbi considered as he poured some iced tea into his glass, the ice cubes softly clinking next to each other. "Well, I might express it a bit differently, but, yes, I think that was essentially what was happening inside Einstein."

"How was he able to sustain that level of concentration? Why was he so obsessed?" I asked.

"On the simplest level, I think it was because he never lost this sense of radical amazement."

Wonder, engagement, and profound abstraction—how could these states co-exist? The question wasn't that, I realized. "How can we keep this sense of amazement? How do we stop it from being lost?"

The rabbi paused. "That is the question, isn't it, Joseph? What do you know of the Kabbalah?"

"Not much," I admitted, ashamed at how I had mastered my

college studies but had a child's knowledge, at best, of Judaism.

"Well, in essence, the Kabbalists say that reality on the simplest level gives hints of another reality beyond what we see."

"Did you ever talk with Einstein about the Kabbalah?"

"Yes, as a matter of fact, I did. Einstein sometimes attended our synagogue if we needed a tenth person for the daily minyan, the quorum needed to recite certain prayers. One day, when services were over, we were talking about science and religion. I quoted Rabbi Mordecai Kaplan: 'The Kabbalists and mystics were aiming at exactly same goal as the scientists and inventors of today ... Kabbalah is the transition between ancient magic and modern science ... the scientist of today is the son of the mystic of yesterday and the grandson of the medicine man of the day before.' This got Albert's attention and he asked me to tell him more about Kabbalah. Albert and I were going to talk as we walked, but a storm blew in and we ducked into a restaurant for coffee.

"I told Albert that the Kabbalists start, as do all Jews, with the Torah, or more specifically with the giving of the Torah at Mount Sinai. But what, exactly, happened on Sinai? There is a wonderful Hassidic teaching that asks: What did Moses really hear? Was it the whole Torah? Just the Ten Commandments? Just the First Commandment? Just the first word of the First Commandment? Or perhaps just the first letter of the first word?

"'But that's aleph, which is silent,' said Mr. Grunfest, one of the congregants who had come along with us.

"'Exactly,' I replied, 'and that's the problem—or rather the lesson. Moses had to translate that silence into human language. Even Maimonides, the great medieval philosopher, says about the Revelation at Sinai, 'We believe that the Torah has reached Moses from God in a manner which is figuratively described in Scripture by the term "word," and that nobody has ever known how that took place except Moses himself.' So we are left with Moses' translation of that silence. Part of what Kabbalah attempts to do is to retrieve that Silence, to break through the doors of perception to that silence.

"By then the rain was coming down so hard that I had to speak a little louder to be heard. Rabbi Arziel of Gerona, I explained, expands this concept, teaching, 'Everything visible and perceivable to human contemplation is limited.' That which is not limited, is absolutely undifferentiated in a complete and changeless unity, is called Ein-Sof, or 'Without End.' This is one of the names in Kabbalah for God. If God is without limit, then nothing exists outside of God, and therefore God is the essence of all that is concealed and revealed."

I thought of my grandfather and the Sh'ma. "Hear, O Israel, the Lord is our God, the Lord is one," I chanted to the rabbi.

"Precisely," he exclaimed. "You have had a teacher?"

"My grandfather," I said. "When I was a child, but he died a few years ago."

"I'm sorry. I'm sure if he gave you that teaching he knew that the depth of the message in the Sh'ma is too often lost. Kabbalah is a means to recover our awareness of that primary unity. For Kabbalists, all change requires a return to that point. Albert seemed particularly interested in this idea."

"I'm not sure I understand," I said.

"One of the most important texts of Kabbalah, 'Sefer Yetzirah,' explains that it is the abyss which becomes visible in the gaps of existence. In each transformation of reality, in every change of form, or every time the status of a thing is altered, the abyss of nothingness is crossed and for a fleeting moment becomes visible. Think of your breathing. There is a moment that is neither inhaling nor exhaling. It is like the rest note in a piece of music where nothing happens. That pause is essential for the composition."

"I don't quite understand what that has to do with why Einstein never lost his sense of wonder and awe?"

The rabbi peered at me, "You are good at staying focused on a topic; just the kind of mind that would be very good following the stream-of-consciousness discussions in the Talmud. Have you ever thought of applying your fine young mind to our tradition? Studying for the rabbinate?"

I blushed, as though something very private of mine had been exposed, and tried to respond but could not speak.

The rabbi gazed at me. The lines of his fine, narrow face were severe and if there was compassion in his dark brown eyes it was buried way down, beneath a truth and a commitment that admitted no subterfuge and no evasion. It was like a wall that I had come up against. There was no place left to go. I had the feeling of being trapped, of suffocation.

"Cat got your tongue?" Eden said with a playfulness that defused the moment and allowed me to breathe.

"Please, Eden, let me continue," the rabbi said, still peering at me to let me know that I was not off the hook. A warm conspiratorial connection lingered between the rabbi's wife and me. It made me feel ready to scale the wall, or just crumple beneath it ... I wasn't sure which.

"One warm summer night, Eden and I were strolling down Nassau Street," the rabbi said, "when we bumped into Albert, who was wearing his usual garb, a sweatshirt and baggy khakis. He was walking with a visitor, one of the destitute refugees from Europe whom he frequently put up in his house despite his desire for solitude to work. And, by the way, there was rarely a day that went by when someone didn't barge in on him: physicists, philosophers, theologians, Zionists, writers, journalists, artists, and refugees. Sometimes he would sneak through the bushes in his backyard and hide out in the home of his next-door neighbor, Dr. Eric Rogers, to escape attention.

"Albert introduced us to this particular refugee, Andrew, a recently arrived physics student from Germany. A discussion started about how movies are really optical illusions. Think about it: What is a movie? Still photos projected on a screen in a way that makes them seem to be moving pictures, when, in fact, they are still photos. I mentioned to Albert that this was analogous to the Kabbalistic insights that I had previously tried to explain to him. Not following my point, Albert, with some impatience, asked me to elaborate.

"'If life was like a movie,' I replied, 'and we were able to slow it down, we would see the blank spaces between each frame. Because of the speed of the individual picture frames flashed on the screen, we normally don't see the blank spaces. Kabbalah is a system where we try to see those spaces.'"

"How did he respond?" I asked.

"He asked me to explain further, so I told him that while seeing the 'blank spaces' is a part of training in Kabbalah, it is not a place where initiates dwell. Just as we would go crazy watching a movie in which we saw every empty space all the time, we would also go crazy if we constantly apprehended the empty blank silent spaces between the moments of existence. To shield us from that silence, God is refracted like light through a prism into what the Kabbalists called the ten sefirot, the ten basic units of reality, the dramatic emanation of God in this world. Albert perked up when he heard this. The lowest level is Malchut, which means kingship, and is also known as Shechinah, a feminine name that can best be understood as divine presence—a junction where the Divine can be experienced in this world. Kabbalists try to experience the world through higher levels than most of us. This is done through the withdrawal from the physical world; enabling one to expand the frontiers of consciousness into what Jung would say is the 'universal unconscious.' Some might say it is related to the Eyn Sof of Kabbalah.

"At that point, Albert reminded me that he and Jung had been friends in Zurich, and that on a number of occasions he had been Jung's dinner guest. They discussed what was then his developing theory of relativity, which Jung would later acknowledge in his own theory of synchronicity. Jung wrote: 'Synchronicity takes the coincidence of events in space and time as meaning something more than mere chance, namely, a peculiar interdependence of objective events among themselves as well as the subjective psychic state of the observer or observers.'"

Caught up in the rabbi's words, I almost didn't hear Eden ask me to pass the Challah. She took a piece, smeared it with olive spread, and gave it to me. The rabbi returned to my question about Einstein's sense of wonder. "Let me share with you something Albert once wrote," said the rabbi, pulling a sheet of paper from the folder. "'We are in the position of a child entering a huge library, whose walls are covered to the ceiling with books in many different languages. The child knows that someone must have written those books. He or she does not know who or how. He or she does not understand the languages in which they are written. The child notes a definite plan in the arrangement of the books, a mysterious order, which he or she does not comprehend but only dimly suspects.'"

"I have occasionally sensed that mysterious order," I said. "But I have always felt myself step back from the edge."

The rabbi nodded. "I understand your hesitation. But one of the tasks of a religious mind is to sustain this sense and feeling. I believe Albert was able to hold on to it by stepping into those silent blank spaces of the universe because of his neshama, his soul. Each of us has a neshama, our unique spiritual link to the world and the universe.

"I can see by the look on your face that I need to flesh this out. Let me try," he said, taking a breath. "All living creatures have a soul, a nefesh, that spark of the source of life. Humans also have a ruach, perhaps best translated as spirit. It is that which separates us from other living creatures."

"And how is that?" I asked.

"It is our awareness that we have a soul, a nefesh. As far as we know, other living creatures don't have that awareness."

"How else are we different?"

"We have a historical memory beyond our own life. We understand the concept of humor. And we have an awareness, early on in our lives, that we will die. All of these shape our lives as human beings—as should our acting upon our knowledge that we have a soul. Acting upon that awareness is called having a neshama, also meaning soul, but perhaps soul awareness is better. One of our challenges of life, one of our most important goals, is to develop our neshama to its fullest; it is what makes us more fully human and alive. Joseph, how do you develop your soul? What classes are you taking at university to help you to that end?"

I heard him ask that question in a way that was a challenge to how I was living my life. All that I stood for, a comfortable white middle-class suburban lifestyle that had sent me to university so I could learn—that is, so I could learn to succeed economically. Where was my soul in that equation? Where was any Judaism in that equation? He had touched a raw nerve, even if I agreed with his point, and so I shot back. "If all this Jewish learning is so important and insightful, why did six million Jews not see the Holocaust coming and leave?!"

"Ah, there is some life in you. So you are not just going to let me spoon-feed this to you. Good, Joseph, you raise a very complex question, which we can perhaps return to at some other time. All I will say is that it has less to do with the failure of Jews to, as you said, see it coming, and more to do with one of the centers of Western civilization turning off its soul and allowing itself to become a monster. For now let us return to the question of the development of the soul.

"We are reminded of this every morning by the Siddur, the prayer book, when we ask ourselves eight existential questions that begin, 'mah anachnu, meh chayenu—What are we? What is our life?' That is to say, What are we going to do to develop this marvelous gift of ours, our God-given soul, to its fullest? How would you answer that question now, Joseph?"

I looked to Eden, but this time she was quiet, inspecting me with a kind of curious and distant regard.

"Rabbi," I said, this time not feeling attacked, but hearing his question in a different light, "I can't answer that question yet, but I want to be able to."

"Wanting is not always enough, Joseph," said the rabbi.

I was puzzled and a bit hurt. Why wasn't wanting enough? The rabbi gazed at me, waiting. But, once again, I stepped back from the brink. "Most of us seem to lose that wonder as we get older," I said. "Are there ways that we can hold on to it?"

"The Hebrew word for holy is kodesh," the rabbi responded. "Kodesh, at its core, also means 'to divide' and 'to separate.' When we usually think about holiness, we think about the interconnectedness of things." The rabbi wagged a finger at me, indicating that he wanted me to hear very clearly what he was about to say. "But before we can relate to the 'oneness,' the 'unity of the world,' we must first see all the holy separate parts of the world. This is why we say so many blessings each day: blessings for seeing an ocean, rainbow, lightning, shooting stars, a tree, a blossom, hearing thunder, smelling spices. We must really see, appreciate, and recognize all the separate parts. Only then can we really experience them as part of a greater whole. To be aware of this varied mosaic of life the rabbis tell us in the Talmud that we should say a minimum of a hundred blessings a day. This places one in a state of thanks. The name Jew comes from Judah, or Yehudah, the fourth son of Leah and Jacob, whose name means thanks. The essence of a Jew is to live a life thankful for what one has. That is a very powerful outlook to have that can make the 'burdens' of life easier to carry as well."

"Is there a blessing for seeing a wise person?" I asked.

"Yes," answered the rabbi, "... shenatan mechochmato levasar vadam, which means, 'Who bestowed upon mortals some of Your glory.' I used to tease Albert sometimes when I saw him by saying that blessing, and we'd have a good laugh! Albert had a great sense of humor. For his seventy-fifth birthday he was given a parrot named Bibo. When Einstein thought the parrot was depressed, he would tell jokes to it."

The mood in the room was light, but under it I realized I was trembling with a kind of keen anticipation. The rabbi had awakened a hunger in me with his explanation of separateness and wholeness.

"What is a blessing, exactly?" I asked.

"A good question," said the rabbi. "The Hebrew word for blessing is bracha. It is related to the word breecha, which means pool. Think about the feeling that you get on a hot, humid day when you jump into a mountain stream. You feel alive, refreshed, and aware as the cool water envelops you. That's what a bracha is: to really notice and be aware of the moment, what I understand the Buddhists call mindfulness. This feeling is similar to Einstein's 'rapturous amazement at the harmony of natural law.'" The rabbi pulled a letter from his folder and read from its dark black typed letters: "'I am of the opinion that all the finer speculations in the realm of science spring from a deeper religious feeling, and that without such feeling they would not be fruitful ... The most beautiful and most profound emotion we can experience is the sensation of the mystical. It is the sower of all true science. He to whom this emotion is a stranger, who can no longer wonder and stand rapt in awe, is as good as dead. To know that what is impenetrable to us really exists, manifesting itself as the highest wisdom and the most radiant beauty which our dull faculties can comprehend only in their most primitive forms—this knowledge, this feeling, is at the center of true religiousness ... My religion consists of a humble admiration of the illimitable superior spirit who reveals Himself in the slight details we are able to perceive with our frail and feeble minds. That deeply emotional conviction of the presence of a superior reasoning power, which is revealed in the incomprehensible universe, forms my idea of God.'"

Eden then reminded the rabbi that his doctor insisted that he take an afternoon nap every day.

The rabbi sighed. "You're right. I must nap. Let's bentsch, say our prayers after eating, and then I'll see our friend to the door."

It was with a sharp sense of regret that I stood on the rabbi's front porch. He was the teacher I had been looking for, and I was loath to leave.

"Rabbi," I said wanting to extend our time together. "You don't seem detached from the real world, and yet you're also full of Jewish knowledge. How are you able to ... I can't find the right words."

"Live in two civilizations simultaneously."

"Yes, that's it."

"When you come back next from college I will tell you."

My heart sang as I nodded assent.

"Don't be too happy," he said as he saw my face light up. "I have not forgotten my question to you."

41

I had not forgotten it either. He held out his hand. I shook it and turned my steps toward home.

# 8

## Corina

My discussion with the rabbi followed me back to college like an unfinished sonata looking for completion. His question about what I was doing with my life played over and over in my mind. I started to make changes in increments in my life. Changes with results I did not expect.

In the fall I had taken an art history class. Corina Contessa, a junior, sat in front of me the first day of class. Soon we began to flirt, and then entered that haze of falling in love, when all of one's thoughts are taken up anticipating the next time you will see the one you desire. When seeing each other in the art history was not enough we began to make time for each other outside of class.

That semester we spent hours talking about art, politics, and philosophy, as well as going to many movies on campus, shown in one of the large science lecture halls. It was not uncommon for us to join my roommate Billy Shears for late-night conversations in the pottery studio. Often the conversations would drift toward questions of theology. Billy was a lapsed Catholic and Corina was a Unitarian. And then there was me—Jewish, but not firmly grounded in what that meant. Those late-night conversations made me further realize I needed to resolve—to clarify—what my Jewish identity meant, both in terms of thought and deed.

While I shared a dorm room with Billy, I spent most of my time in Corina's off-campus apartment at the bottom of Loomis Street. On Saturday mornings we would mix and knead flour, water, and yeast together. With the smell of fermenting yeast filling her small one-bedroom apartment as it rose, we would make love. Hiking in rain-soaked forests colored by the fall foliage eventually gave way to late-night walks through the muffled streets of Burlington as the snow fell.

We were in love and I looked forward to the spring. After I came back from meeting the rabbi for the first time, I told Corina all about him. There was animation in my voice when I spoke about him and what we had discussed. Corina and I added those issues to our conversations.

"Okay, Joseph," Corina said one evening as we had dinner at Bove's Restaurant, "let's think this through logically. You said the rabbi said, for Einstein there was no difference between religious and scientific problems. That Einstein called God 'the presence of a superior reasoning power.'"

"Exactly," I said, thinking there was nothing else to add or explore. Corina said that my thinking had become less critical since I had met the rabbi. I did not realize it then, but I had started on a journey that would soon not include Corina. But I did not know any of that then, as I buttered a warm piece of bread. Corina continued. "It may sound nice, but what does it really mean?"

"Corina, remember what we learned last semester in Art History about how Michelangelo painted the robe surrounding God in the Creation of Adam for the Sistine Chapel to look like the silhouette of a brain to signify the Medieval philosophical notion of God as pure thought and reason."

"Okay, I'll grant you that, but it still does not get around the issue of God as a supernatural God, that is to say a God who can mess with nature at whim. Einstein certainly did not believe that. If you say that Einstein did not believe in a supernatural God then you have redefined God so much that you are not really talking about God."

"I need to think about that," I said as I twirled my pasta in the white wine and clam sauce.

"That's right, don't forget to think," she said with a smile.

Soon things really began to change; a distance began to grow between us. More and more my speech was framed as opinion; my emotions, my feelings toward Corina began to fade. I slept over one Friday night at Corina's as I normally did. When she started to get the flour, water, and yeast ready to make bread the next morning I said, "Not today."

"But, Joseph," she said putting her hands around my waist, "this is our ritual." I lifted my head and looked beyond her for a moment and then said, "I need to start being more Jewish."

She released her hands from around my waist and said, "And what does that mean?"

"I don't know exactly, but the rabbi said something to me in his letter that got me thinking that I need to take my Jewish identity more seriously. I don't know a lot but I know that cooking on Shabbat is not allowed. It's a place to start, and now is the moment."

"And how far are you going to go with this?" she said as her face tensed up. "Wearing a yarmulke? Praying all the time? Eating kosher food? No pre-marital sex?!" The last one she said with a Let's See You Pull That One Off attitude. We then approached each other, embraced, and ended up in bed. Forces beyond our control added to the passion that evening.

# 9

## Early Changes

The next week I returned home to celebrate my parents' wedding anniversary. It also would give me a chance to speak with the rabbi. I was concerned about what was happening to me, like my decisions were being decided somewhere else. Nathan and his family were also visiting. Fortunately my sister-in-law was a vegetarian and so a vegetarian meal was served and I did not have to worry about telling my parents that I would not eat their non-Kosher meat. The thing that got to me was that they were more than happy to accommodate her, but if I had asked that they also serve vegetarian food for reasons of Kashrut it would have been a whole scene.

Even though Nathan was married with two young children, whenever the four of us would get together we would still play quadruple solitaire. And so after dinner the dinning room table was cleared for us to play. As always we played at a fast and furious pace with the usual banter between us. Afterwards I started to go though some of the boxes behind the green curtain downstairs where my parents had things stored from their past. I found a box with "Wedding" written across it. I opened it and found a cardboard tube and a white wedding photo album. I ran upstairs saying, "Look what I found."

I sat down next to my parents and pulled out a piece of

paper, with lots of Hebrew writing on it, from the tube. "What is it?" my parents asked.

I looked at it for a short while and then realized that it was their Ketubah, the traditional Jewish wedding document.

"I completely forgot that we had one of those," my mother said.

We then started looking through the wedding album. After a while I noticed that my grandfather, Zayda, was not in any of the photos. "Mom, why are there no photos of Zayda?"

In a quick and terse voice she said, "He had a very bad cold." I thought that was a bit odd but did not make too much of it at the time. That night when I went to sleep I picked up one of my father's history books. I always loved to read his notes written in his distinctive compact handwriting in margins or at the end of chapters. That night I read Edmund Wilson's To The Finland Station: A Study in the Writing and Acting of History. At the end of the first chapter my father had written, "What Michelet discovered through Vico: the realization of the interrelatedness of the elements that make up history—and that underlying it all is some sort of universal natural law."

The next day I went to see the rabbi. It was still unseasonably warm and sunny. The rabbi said that he was happy to see me so soon. We sat out on the front porch, shaded by a pine tree; a slight cool breeze kept us comfortable. The rabbi looked over his shoulder back into the house to make sure Eden wasn't around. My heart beat more quickly. Was he going to divulge some private information?

"I was born in 1907," he said, "and we lived on the Upper West Side of Manhattan in a Jewish neighborhood filled with synagogues, Talmud Torahs, Jewish religious schools, kosher butchers, and Jewish book sellers. My parents had moved there from the lower East Side—a move for them, as well as many others, from the ratty tenements of new immigrants to a neighborhood that housed a growing Jewish middle class."

"My own grandparents made similar journeys," I said.

"What courage they had," said the rabbi. "What perseverance and hope! I often went to Oheb Zedek across the street from my school," he continued, "where we would hear the great chazzan Yosele Rosenblatt. His voice was of such a quality that the Metropolitan Opera had offered him a job, but he turned it down because he would have had to work on Shabbat. My parents sent me to a Talmud Torah from the age of three until I was six. Then I entered public school."

"But that was not the end of your Jewish education?"

"Of course not! Jewish education was all-important to my parents. They were students of the Haskalah, the Jewish enlightenment, however, and wanted my education to be as broad as possible. I attended public school, but they made sure that I had the best private Jewish tutors they could find—two hours every Monday, Tuesday and Thursday afternoon. Three hours each Sunday morning."

"That's serious learning."

"I loved it! My tutors challenged me. They made me think, they helped me develop a point of view, as well as enriched my life."

I thought of my classes at college. I did well in them; they made me think, but did my life have more meaning because of them? "Did your secular studies clash with what you learned from your tutors or heard in synagogue?" I asked.

"It's ironic, but it was at a synagogue that my first serious questions, doubts, I should say, were raised. The synagogue, Ansche Chesed, was then located on 114th Street and Seventh Avenue. Up until that point in my life, I had only been to Orthodox Shuls. This one was Conservative. A few weeks after I became Bar-Mitzvah, I went to services there. Rabbi Jacob Kohn was not only knowledge-able in Talmud and Midrash. That morning in his drash, his sermon, he spoke about Freud, Marx, and Einstein! It was exciting to listen to someone weave the religious and the secular with so much natural ease and depth. Soon afterwards, I joined the youth group there."

"How did your parents react?"

"They were more fearful that the attractions of secular American culture would pull me away from Judaism, so even though the synagogue wasn't Orthodox, they didn't try to dissuade me. Still, I couldn't share everything that I was thinking with them."

"What do you mean?"

"My world view of Torah min Ha-Shamayim, Torah as a divinely given book, was shattered. My belief in God never wavered, but my understanding of God as a supernatural Being was challenged, and I did not know what to replace it with.

"For years I was torn by an inner conflict. I would muddle my answers to my parents and tutors when they asked about my emunah, my faith."

I felt humbled that the rabbi would share such a personal story with me. I thought of my own parents and others and wondered if I would ever feel the need not to tell them what I really felt, if what I felt or thought ran counter to their beliefs.

"But rabbi, if your belief in Torah as a divinely given book had been shattered and that is one of the foundations of Judaism, then how can you say that your understanding of God is authentic?"

"Joseph, this is an important point," the rabbi said, leaning closer to me. "Never confuse belief in God with an understanding of who or what God is. Don't fall into the trap, that confusion."

Eden emerged from the house and told the rabbi that they had to get ready for his doctor's appointment. I was disappointed that this visit was so short. I had not had time to tell him about how

I had started to observe Shabbat and other changes that I was making in my life.

"Just a minute, Eden," the rabbi said with a touch of impatience. "The doctor can wait."

"How sick are you, rabbi?" I blurted out. I was suddenly afraid he would die before whatever knowledge I was searching for from him would be imparted.

The hardness was back in his eyes as he looked at me again. "Good, Joseph, good. You see, wanting is different than needing. Needing is something you can't live without. Wanting? There are many teachers out there; there are many links in the chain going back to Moses and Abraham. If I die tomorrow it doesn't matter."

His words confused me. Perhaps he was only the medium, the conduit. But I was beginning to feel a deep connection to him.

"It's not that, rabbi," I said. He could hear the feeling in my voice.

"I know," he said, laying his hand upon my head. "When will you return again from school?"

"I'll be home for Passover."

"Please call," said the rabbi. "I give my word that I'll do my best to be here!" With that, he laughed. "Shabbat Shalom," he said and walked slowly back into the house, leaning heavily on Eden's arm. I was also very disappointed. I needed to talk to him about Corina and the other changes that were going on in my life.

My parents did not show much interest in my meetings with the rabbi. While at first they thought that I had tried to find the rabbi because of my long-standing curiosity about Einstein, now, I think they deliberately chose to remain silent about what they must have clearly seen as the source of differences they began to notice in me. I suppose they were hoping it was just a phase, and it would pass.

Nonetheless, my mother did have something she wanted to give me when I returned from my visit with the rabbi.

"Joseph, your finding the wedding album reminded me that I had stored something else away that I had forgotten to give you. When Zayda died, as he requested we had him buried with his talis. He explained to me that for it to buried one of the bundles of strings needed to be cut off."

"Mom they're called tzizit."

"He asked that I give it to you. In all the intensity following his death I forgot to give them to you."

She then handed me a plain white envelope with "For Joseph" written on it. I could feel the knots of tzizit inside. I opened the envelope and held the woven strings in my hand. Tears welled in my eyes. I hugged my mother and ran up to my bedroom. I took out my talis and tied the tzizit to one of the tzizit on one of the corners of my talis. They remain there to this day. When I hold them, I also hold my Zayda.

# 10

## Riding on a Beam of Light

I returned to the University of Vermont in Burlington the following week. Northern Vermont was still in the throes of winter. The city was buffeted by west winds. Frigid air, chilled first in the Adirondack Mountains, raced across frozen Lake Champlain. I would fall asleep thinking of the rabbi and Einstein and Kabbalah and then dream about the David. The statue came toward me in the echoing hall. But now I didn't run. I was rooted where I stood, unable to move. I'd wake, trembling, filled with a strange energy, and walk down in the middle of the night to the frozen lake, where I'd look up at the glistening stars and listen to the ice groan its deep primordial groan.

One day in the library I came across a book on Einstein with a photo in it of him at the Oranienburgerstrasse Synagogue in Berlin in 1930. The book also mentioned that Einstein had a photograph of a portrait of Michelangelo in his office.

I kept wondering what Einstein was doing at that synagogue? Did he pray? Attend services? My visit with the rabbi had sparked so much curiosity in me that I did not want to wait two months to continue our conversation. I decided to write him a short letter and ask him about the photo and Michelangelo.

Each day, I opened my mailbox, waiting for a reply. A yellow envelope soon appeared, addressed to me in a spindly hand. With great excitement I sat down in the common area by a large window. Snow was falling outside, muting everything, softening and enclosing it, and heightening the air of intimacy that is often present when opening and reading a letter.

*Dear Joseph,*

*It was so good of you to write. The photo that you are speaking of in the Oranienburgerstrasse Synagogue in Berlin was taken when Albert was there to give a violin concert. Einstein loved to play Mozart. Music was his refuge. Albert once told me that the music of Mozart "was so pure that it seemed to have been ever-present in the universe, waiting to be discovered by the master." I'm sure you can appreciate the affinity. Both Mozart and Albert were not trying to discover something new. They both worked at revealing those harmonies of the universe that have been there since the beginning of time.*

    *As for Michelangelo ... I think you noticed the photo of Michelangelo's David in my study. Michelangelo would study a piece of marble and see the figure that he would eventually carve—liberating or revealing the form in the stone, in the same way Bach revealed harmonies or Einstein's equations revealed the architecture of the cosmos.*

    *Albert once commented to me that although the statue of David was indeed impressive, he was more intrigued by the four statues of the "Prisoners" located in the big hall of the Galleria dell'Academia that leads the visitor to the David. He showed me that if you look closely on the top of one of them you can see three interconnected rings. That was Michelangelo's signature, a request for that particular piece of marble to be sent from the quarry in Carrara to his studio. The four prisoners were intended to be used for the tomb of Pope Julius II. But the tomb was never completed. Michelangelo's Moses in Rome's San Pietro In Vincoli was also to be part of that tomb.*

    *Of course that was the famous statue of Moses with the two horns coming out of his head. We read from Vasari, who was a contemporary of Michelangelo, in his famous "Lives of the Artists," that "the Jews are to be seen every Saturday, or on their Sabbath, hurrying like a flight of swallows, men and women, to visit and worship this figure, not as a work of the human hand, but as something divine." Albert asked me about the horns. Raised in Europe, he was familiar with the notion that Jews had horns and it was not uncommon to see other statues of Moses or of Jews from the Middle Ages and Renaissance with horns. I explained to him that all of that was based on a mistranslation of the Hebrew. There is even an example of that not far from here on the Princeton campus on the back wall relief of Alexander Hall.*

    *The Hebrew text says that "when Moses came down from Mount Sinai with the two tablets of Testimony in Moses' hand, when he came down from the mountain, Moses did not know that the skin of* his face was radiating light rays because of Moses having spoken with God (Exodus 34:29)." The Hebrew for "light ray" is keren, which can also mean "horn." When the Bible was translated into Latin, the Vulgate, by Jerome in the fourth century, he mistranslated the word keren as "horn" and not "light ray." This in and of itself is not that remarkable, but it would add one more proof—text to those who held anti-Semitic views, since it tied Jews to the horned Devil.

Albert was intrigued by the statues of the "Prisoners" because while they were not "finished," they felt to him in many ways complete as the prisoners struggle to emerge out of the Carrara marble, frozen in the act of becoming. I asked him why he felt that way. He replied that he was drawn to the notion of something being complete.

Nothing is ever totally complete, he said. There are only stages along the way. Knowledge, he said, is a process in constant motion, frozen for a moment with each new discovery, only to break through— like the figures in the marble—to the next discovery. For example, he reminded me that his 1907 discovery of the Principle of Equivalence, which stated that the effects of gravity and accelerated motion are the same, eventually led in 1916 to his discovery of the General Theory of Relativity.

Once a student asked him, "Why are the questions on this year's exam the same as last year's?" Albert replied, "This year all the answers are different."

In September 1940 I attended a Conference on Science, Philosophy, and Religion in New York City that had been organized by my friend Rabbi Louis Finkelstein who was then President of the Jewish Theological Seminary. Albert and I took the train together from Princeton. While on the train we discussed Michelangelo. I mentioned to Albert that Michelangelo was twenty-six when he carved the David and he was twenty-six when he wrote his Special Theory of Relativity. There must be something about twenty-six and the creative process.

Picasso painted his revolutionary cubist painting *Les Demoiselles d'Avignon* and more recently John Lennon co-wrote the groundbreaking Beatles album *Sgt. Pepper's Lonely Hearts Club Band* when they were both twenty-six. 1905 was his *annus mirabilis*, the year he also completed his papers on light quanta showing that light also acts as a particle (called photons). This had major consequences toward a better understanding of quantum physics and led to his being awarded the Nobel Prize in 1921. In 1905 he also wrote about Brownian motion, proving the existence of atoms. And finally that year he also came to the conclusion, by taking Special Relativity a bit further, that $E = mc^2$. Albert gave me a knowing smile. He had a healthy enough view of himself to see a parallel between his capacities and someone as great as Michelangelo. Not only did they both do great, perhaps their greatest, work at 26, but they both connected religion with other disciplines: Einstein with science, Michelangelo with art. Both were questing for truth, stirred to wrestle beyond the corporeal world in which they found themselves, in which we all live. They both felt the Holy Presence, which permeates all. Both needed to understand, translate, and interpret it. Michelangelo's medium was marble and paint; Einstein's, the mathematical equation.

I paused from reading the letter and remembered my art history teacher's comment on Michelangelo's painting of *The Creation of Adam* where the cloth painted as the silhouette of a human brain symbolized God as pure thought. Michelangelo was not just a painter; he was also a theologian. I returned to the letter.

I know that you are searching for your own relationship to Judaism through your fascination with Einstein. I want you to know that Albert strongly identified with Judaism and the Jewish people, although that identity went through different stages. I was not the only rabbi with whom Albert talked. He knew Rabbi Finkelstein and corresponded with other rabbis. He even met the great twentieth-century *teacher Rav Kook, in Israel in 1923. Kook, the first chief Ashkenazi rabbi of Israel, saw the value of secular learning and tried to bridge the secular and religious worlds. Kook told Einstein, as they stood in the front courtyard of Kook's home in the center of Jerusalem, that many dramatic scientific discoveries were already known in the framework of the Kabbalah. Can you imagine what that conversation must have been like?*

*On the one hand, we have Kook, who bridged the Jewish world of the mystical and the rational and tried to unite secular and religious Jews. On the other, we have Einstein, who, as I have mentioned, was intoxicated with the Splendor of the Unknown, but also had his feet firmly planted on the ground—a secular Jew in outward appearance and practice, but deeply spiritual and mystical in thought and outlook.*

*Albert stopped by to see me about a month before Rosh Hashanah in 1935, just after Kook had died. He had been in Princeton for about two years, working at the Institute for Advanced Study, but we had met only once. It was our discussion about Kook that ignited what would become twenty years of conversations. Albert appreciated that I could see that his scientific quest was also a spiritual quest. That became clear to me when we discussed how he and Kook understood light.*

*As a teenager, Einstein would ask himself, 'What would the world look like if I rode a beam of light?' What sweet chutzpah! Einstein as a teenager trying to understand what it would be like to ride a wave of God's light! Kook called his seminal theological work Orot, which means Lights. It was published two years before he and Albert met.*

*Think about the word that we use for spiritual insight— "enlightenment." Most light, like infrared and ultra-violet rays, can't be seen with the naked eye. These kinds of light touch us all the time, yet we don't see them. This is often how it is with God's presence. Remember that on our spiritual journey, even in moments of enlightenment, we experience only a limited aspect of God's totality. It makes so much sense, light and God, light as God's medium in the world. Remember in his Special Theory of Relativity Albert taught us that the speed of light, and not time, is the constant of the Universe. And what are the first words spoken by God? "Let there be light."*

*We often use the word "darkness" as a metaphor for God's absence. Most objects in the world give off no visible light, but we see them because of the light rays that bounce off them from some source of light. The root word of Torah is yarah, to shoot, as in to shoot an arrow, because Torah points us toward how we should live our lives. The Hebrew word for Jewish Law is halacha. At its core, it means "to walk," expressing that the Law and tradition are there to show us how to walk through life. Without God we are in the dark. As we read in the Bible, "They grope in the dark without light, and he makes them stagger like a drunken man" (Job 12:25). And, "Therefore is justice far from us, neither does righteousness overtake us: we wait for light, but behold darkness; for brightness, but we walk in gloom. We grope for the wall like the blind, and we grope as if we had no eyes: we stumble at noonday as in night ..." (Isaiah 59:9-10).*

*You might ask: Why would Einstein have met with Kook? For this we need to understand the maturation of Albert's connection to Judaism. Albert grew up in a typical late nineteenth-century Western European Jewish home. Over the course of the nineteenth century, Jews had emerged from the ghetto. Country after country had said, "Yes, you can be like the rest of us—a voting citizen with rights. Just don't be too Jewish!"*

*For many Jews, this seemed to be a reasonable price to pay after centuries of being "other." But God forbid we should be a shanda fur die goyim! (a disgrace in the eyes of the non-Jew ... an embarrass-*

ment to the Jewish community). Jews began to internalize anti-Semitism. This happens to all groups that are oppressed. Many on a deep level, as persecuted minorities often do, believed all the horrible things that had been said about us for centuries. The nineteenth century offered a new way out of being solely identified as being a Jew. There was now a choice. In the past, if you didn't want to be Jewish, you had to convert out of the religion. Desperate to be accepted, tired of being persecuted and discriminated against, wanting our children to be spared such a fate, many of us became embarrassed by much in the Jewish tradition and began to discard many outward expressions of our Judaism through a process of assimilation.

I thought of my parents and all that our family had forsaken, the shedding of Jewish ritual and observance that had taken place in the three short generations since my great-grandparents had arrived on America's shores. And, yet, even in their secularism, my parents' Jewish identity had remained intact. There was something remarkable about that. I wondered how the rabbi would react to their devout secularism. I knew how they would react to the rabbi's deep connection to Jewish ritual and practice. I sighed, feeling myself caught in the middle of what seemed to be two extremes. I went back to the letter.

Mind you, I am not saying that every innovation was necessarily bad. Judaism has always evolved. At times, though, the change was motivated not by a desire to make Judaism stronger by adapting it to new conditions so that Judaism made more sense for its adherents, but rather by making ourselves less Jewish so that we would be accepted.

There was also that countervailing impulse: those who felt, and still feel, that the tradeoff for acceptance by a lessening of our Jewish identity was too great a price to pay. They completely rejected modernity and assimilation. Too often, however, this desire to see Judaism continue to live in their lives and their children's lives came from a place of *fear rather than joy. It can come not from an internal love of Judaism, but in reaction to external factors that seem bent on destroying Jewish religion and culture.*

*I have somewhat oversimplified a very complex problem, a problem that we are still trying to figure out. I feel for Jews in the world today. How can we live in two civilizations simultaneously? How can we know both our Talmud and baseball or find the Arts and Leisure section of The Sunday New York Times and the Parshat HaShavuah, the weekly Torah section that we read on Shabbat morning with the same ease? Our choices today are in many ways no different from those that Einstein and his family made a century ago.*

*Joseph, my fingers are getting tired, and I still want to tell you about Albert's childhood, which had a great deal to do with his Jewish identity later in life. Since you will be coming home for Pesach, let's carry on our conversation then. Give a call when you get in.*

*Shalom,*

*Asher*

I put the letter down. I was touched and excited that the rabbi had written to me. There was something special about having a letter: Unlike a conversation, the details of which may fade with time, a letter is forever. I longed for more.

The parallels between my own family's Jewish experience and Einstein's family's relationship to Judaism disturbed me. Einstein had somehow managed to integrate his Judaism with the rest of his life. That's what I was looking for. But what was the right balance? Was it to be like Einstein, whose Jewish identity did not include living life as a ritual-observing Jew? Or was it to strive to be more like the rabbi, whose Judaism was marked by constant ritual and who also seemed to be able to bridge the rational and religion? That night I dreamt the dream again: David was striding toward me, holding out his hand, palm up.

# 11

# Billy

Billy and I met when we were roommates our first year at UVM. We have been close friends ever since, with the exception of one period. Being no different from most college students moving into their dorm rooms, we put up pictures and posters that gave us each a sense of home and conveyed to others who we were, and what we stood for. Above my desk I taped "The Trackman's Prayer" by Vincent E. Matthews:

> *Now I lay me down the blocks*
> *I ask the Lord for socks and jocks*
> *If I should die before the gun*
> *I ask the Lord my race be won*

Billy immediately noticed it. "You ran track," he asked.

"Yeah, for six years; from junior high until this past spring," I answered.

The thing about people who run track is the sense of family, or at least it was that way back then when track was still amateur, and money and larger egos had not yet impacted the sport. Unlike other sporting events where opposing sides meet only in the midst of competition, in track & field you stand next to each other talking and joking while waiting for your turn to jump, or throw, or for the next heat.

"You know," Billy said, "according to Einstein's Special Theory of Relativity if I ran for an hour at one-quarter of the speed of light and you were timing me, when I finished your clock would say one hour, but my clock would say 59.40 minutes, a change of one percent. Kind of makes you wonder what a track record really is."

I looked at him with a slight tilt to my head and said, "You know a lot about Einstein?"

"I'm a physics major, so Einstein comes with the territory."

"Hmmm."

"Is that important to you?"

"Yeah, I've had an interest in Einstein since I was a kid. That one about time changing—I hear and understand the words 'How fast you go changes time,' but I don't get it."

This was the first of many conversations we have had over the years about Einstein. He explained to me, "First of all, you need to wipe away the notion that there is something like Universe Standard Time that everyone can set their watches to and say what the time is. It simply does not exist. Einstein came to this conclusion when he realized that the speed of light is a constant of the universe—not time, distance, energy or mass."

"And what does that have to do with time not being an absolute?"

"Because both can't be absolute. Let's say there is a beam of light that travels between points a and b and it takes 10 seconds, but then let's have points a and b move to their right while this is happening and we see that it still takes 10 seconds for the light to move from point a to b. What's the problem here? It takes 10 seconds for the light to move from a to b while they are stationary, and it also takes the same amount of time while they are moving to the right. However, when they move to the right they are also traveling a greater distance. How can it take the same amount of time when one has farther to go and they are traveling at the same speed? Logically we would think that the light has to go faster, but it doesn't, or rather it can't, since as Einstein said, the speed of light is constant. Therefore what must change is time. It still takes a second but that second is not the same time relatively speaking."

Physics and track brought us together, but my religious quest, for a while, put a serious strain on our relationship. It ended my relationship with Corina, and almost did us in as well.

It started sometime during our second semester after I met Rabbi Ternifka. Billy would push me on the whole question of science and religion, saying that I was trying to square a circle. I said that he understood religion in a very limited and narrow definition.

Billy completely supported my spiritual quest at first, though with his Catholic upbringing he didn't always understand what I was doing. So he would sometimes ask me to explain why I was doing what I was doing. He learned a lot about food that semester.

One day he noticed four sets of strings hanging out from under my shirt. "What are those?!" he asked.

"Tzizit. We are told to wear them in the Torah."

"You have got to be kidding. It's one thing to wear a yarmulke. It's one thing to start eating kosher. It's one thing to pray three times a day. But to look like a marionette who's all tied up! Joseph, when is this going to end?!"

"A marionette!"

"Yeah, that's what you've become—a marionette of God. It's like you want God to control your entire life so you don't have to make any decisions yourself."

"You're just jealous because you can't find any spiritual meaning in your Catholicism."

"Is that what you really think? Oh yeah, the Jews, God's

chosen people, who have all the answers. Give me a break. You're probably going to say next semester we can't be roommates since you don't want to be infected by any non-Jewish influences. That's right; go make your own little Joseph the Jew Ghetto. Go fuck yourself!"

With that I slammed the door and stormed out. The next day I moved all my stuff out. Only later in the semester did we reconnect and reconcile what had passed.

# 12

## Secrets

It's a problem when the Passover Seder you're at is not the Seder where you want to be. I had long felt this way about our family Seder, with its cursory ritual and manic pace. So it was with great reluctance that, when I called the rabbi during my week of Spring break, I declined an invitation to come to his home for the Seder.

I declined the rabbi's invitation because I did not want to hurt my parents' feelings and from a fear that I couldn't quite put into words. The thought of going to a rabbi's house for the holiday felt like both a defection and an admission. And something inside me resisted immersing myself too deeply in the rabbi's tightly structured world of ritual even though I was beginning to take on such an identity. I made plans, instead, to visit him for lunch.

Eden greeted me at the door with a wry smile on her face.

"Joseph, Gut Yontif," she said and gave me a kiss and a pat on the cheek, which was almost a playful slap. "I was disappointed that you declined our invitation."

"I was disappointed, too," I replied.

"*Nu*? So what is all this disappointment about?"

I was at a loss. "Asher is a bit tired today," she continued smoothly. "Our Seder lasted until one in the morning, and then he went to services this morning. He pushes himself too hard. I keep telling him that he needs to take care of his heart. I think that he may be taking an early nap in his chair in his office."

We walked down the hall together and peered into his study. The rabbi was covered in his white wool shawl, sitting back in a leather recliner, slippered feet up on its footrest. I hated to disturb him. "I'm awake," he said, opening his eyes. "I learned this trick at yeshiva, where we would always study late into the night. A short quick nap and I'm as good as gold. Joseph, Gut Yontif. It was so nice to get your letter, but it is even nicer to see you here."

I basked in his obvious pleasure at my presence. We sat down for lunch. The rabbi recited the special Kiddush for the day, and then we said the hamotzi over matzoh. We began with a delicious soup. Eden said that she made the broth; Asher, the matzoh balls.

"How was your Seder?" Eden asked, mischief in her voice. I told her that it was fine. I didn't mention that my father had us skip large sections of the service so we could finish in time for him to watch the NBA Playoff Game. I also didn't mention that when we hastily covered the child mentioned in the Haggadah who sets himself apart from the Jewish people, I wondered how my parents could fail to see themselves so described. Or, for that matter, the rest of the people at the table, my aunts and uncles, my siblings and my cousins, none of whom approached the Seder as a rite of celebration and philosophical discussion that connected generations present and past. They weren't interested in the depth of the conversation; just how quickly the meal would be served. When I had suggested that we look at an interesting commentary on the development of the four questions, my cousin said, "Joe, give us a break. You can't make something that is old, irrelevant, sexist, and boring, meaningful and interesting." I didn't mention how my blood boiled at that point and that I almost got up and left.

As I thought about the tensions inside my own family, I wondered about Einstein's family life. Rather than expose my own disappointments and frustrations, I asked the rabbi whether Einstein's family life was a happy one.

Eden's face had a small hard smile that was all-too-knowing, and the rabbi, too polite, did not acknowledge my rather transparent associative process. Rather, he pondered. "Albert once said to me, 'Marriage is the unsuccessful attempt to make something lasting out of an incident.' Unfortunately I think that is a fair assessment of how he viewed marriage. Einstein's first marriage to Mileva ended in divorce, and, while I hate to say this, I believe that, on some level, the death of his second wife, Elsa, with whom he had become involved while he was still married to Mileva, was a relief to him."

"Did you ever speak to him about it?"

"No. Eden thought that I should have, but anything I said would only have annoyed him. Don't get the impression that Albert was incapable of love. He and his oldest son, Hans, were close. They both shared common interests in sailing and music. They played duets, Hans on the piano, Einstein on the violin. Hans immigrated to the United States in 1938 and eventually became Professor of Hydraulic Engineering at the University of California. Albert also had a soft spot for his younger son, Eduard, who was both talented and sensitive but eventually developed schizophrenia and lived most of his life with Mileva.

"It was with his sister, Maja, his step-daughter, Margot, and his secretary, Helen Dukas, that his sense of family love showed. Lily Kahler, a friend of ours, once said about Albert and his sister that they were '...,two old people sitting together with their bushy hair, in complete agreement, understanding and love.' He was devoted to her. She lived with him at Mercer Street from 1939 until her death in 1951. He read to her every night at her bedside after she had her stroke. With Margot he shared an interest in art and nature. Later in life he also developed a relationship with Johanna Fantova, whom he had known previously in Europe. Johanna enjoyed cooking him weinershnitzel and in many ways reminded him of the soulfulness and intelligence of pre-war Europe, which, I believe, he missed."

The conversation turned to Einstein and his childhood, which is where the rabbi had left off in his letter. Eden stood up and opened one of the bay windows slightly. The smells of the warming earth and the sounds of birdsong drifted into the dining room, reminding us that Passover is a holiday of spring and rebirth.

"Being freethinkers," the rabbi began, serving himself some Salad Nicoise, "Einstein's parents rejected religion, but Einstein was drawn to religious questions about the ultimate nature of the universe. This kind of questioning was an early example of his nonconformist ways." The rabbi looked at me with his piercing, speculative gaze. "Einstein's father regarded most of the Jewish customs and traditions as ancient superstitions. The family ate pork and other forbidden non-Kosher foods. They did not attend synagogue, but they did keep the Jewish custom of feeding the poor. An indigent Jewish medical student from Russia named Max Talmey ate with them every Thursday night.

"Talmey, though ten years older than Einstein, took a liking to him and introduced Einstein to Kant, Darwin and books on physics. These books exposed Albert to science and led him to re-evaluate his Judaism." The rabbi pulled a typed page from a folder he had placed on a nearby chair, unfolded it, and began to read, "'Through the reading of popular scientific books I soon reached the conviction that much in the stories of the Bible could not be true. The consequence was a positively fanatic orgy of freethinking coupled with the impression that youth is intentionally being deceived by the state through lies; it was a crushing impression. Mistrust of every kind of authority grew out of this experience, a skeptical attitude toward the convictions that were alive in any specific social environment—an attitude that has never again left me.'

"Questioning for Albert was all-important. It was not only the key to knowledge, but also a powerful tool when it came to keeping authority in check. Think of the great rabbis of the Talmud: Rav and Shmuel, Hillel and Shammai were paired off not because they agreed with each other but because they disagreed. They needed, and we need, to be reminded to be open to the voice of the other. Albert's life in many ways was defined by his questions, even if we only remember his answers."

"So you don't think the Bible is entirely true?" I blurted out, afraid I may have crossed a line, but needing to know.

"The Bible may not be all literally true, but it is about Truth." The rabbi paused to allow me to absorb what he had just said. He then continued. "It is the lens through which we Jews see the world, and therein lies its power—and I said as much many times, in many different ways, to Albert."

"How did he respond?"

"His reactions were complex. At lunch one day, we talked about the books that Talmey had introduced him to and his distrust of authority and tradition. Albert confessed to me that he had refused to have a Bar Mitzvah ceremony."

"Did that make him not Jewish?" I asked, a bit worried.

"No, no," chuckled the rabbi. "One reaches the status of Bar Mitzvah automatically. A boy at the age of thirteen becomes responsible for fulfilling the commandments. For girls this status is reached at twelve, since, as we know, they mature before young boys."

"And they continue to stay more mature, despite the fact that boys are sometimes mistakenly called men," said Eden from the kitchen, where she had gone to bring in dessert.

"Unfortunately, she is right," said the rabbi with a smile. "The actual ceremony for a Bar Mitzvah is fairly recent, only about 600 years old. At any rate, Albert rebelled not against religion or the Bible, but against organized religion. In Munich, he was sent to the local Catholic-run school, which he attended until the age of nine. It is interesting that there he saw no great difference between the Catholicism he learned and the vague remnants of his family's Judaism. He once told me, commenting on the fact that he was the only Jewish child in the school, 'This actually worked to my advantage, since it made it easier for me to isolate myself from the rest of the class and find that comfort in solitude that I so cherished.'"

"Why did Einstein like to spend so much time alone, Rabbi?"

"He needed time to think, to work out his ideas. He once told me: 'Sincerely speaking, I have never been much interested in people but only in things.' That was one of the reasons I so cherished the time Albert and I spent together. One summer morning, we took a rowboat out on Carnegie Lake, where we had some of our best conversations. Albert preferred sailing, while I preferred the steadier rowboat. He would tease me that I was afraid of the wind, God's breath. The Princeton crew team glided by in their long slim boats, their oars entering the water to the same rhythmic beat.

Albert said that his Jewish home and classes at the Catholic Peterschule made him feel that the universe obeyed certain laws and that underscoring the world and the universe was a certain harmony."

"Asher," said Eden, "it is a beautiful spring day. Let's bentsch and go for a walk."

The rabbi nodded. We said the blessings for the meal's conclusion and cleared the table. It was early April. Birds were building nests, trees and shrubs were in bloom, and there was a sweet smell in the air. We walked slowly up Pine Street, Eden limping and the rabbi ambling along. "This dogwood tree has begun to blossom," he said, "and I am here for another spring to see it!" They then recited the blessing upon seeing a tree blossom for the first time in the year. "Baruch attah adonai eloheynu meleck ha-olam, she-lo chisar b'o-lamo davar, u-vara vo b'riyot tovot v'ilanot tovim l'hanot ba-shem b'nei adam." Eden translated for me, "Blessed are You, Ruler of the Universe who has withheld nothing from God's world and who has created beautiful creatures and beautiful trees for mortals to enjoy."

They were arm in arm, but, at that moment, Eden reached over and squeezed the rabbi's hand. It was a touch of reassurance, and it made me wonder about the real condition of the rabbi's heart. It is hard for most nineteen-year-olds to comprehend serious illness, and I was no exception. The rabbi stopped, breathed deeply, and closed his eyes for a moment. "This is one of our favorite trees on this street," he said. "It has such a delicate smell when it flowers. Joseph," said the rabbi at that moment, "I am so glad that you sought me out. There is much that I would like to teach you."

"And I would like to learn."

"But there is a potential problem here." My heart sank. The rabbi continued, "I was brought up in a world defined by Judaism, where Jewish knowledge was held on the highest of pedestals. All of that gave me what it takes to create a variation on a theme. But what do you bring to the table, Joseph?"

My heart raced. He's not going to let me in, I thought. He's not going to share with me what he knows. "If not you, then who?" I said in desperation.

"I know you are being sincere, and not trying to falsely flatter me, but you need to understand that there is a masa, a burden, that comes with this knowledge. And the only way to unload that burden is to tell others."

"So tell me."

"Joseph, that is part of the problem. You cannot be told. You must discover. That anger I sensed that you felt at your Seder last night and the anxiety that you feel now are not traits that you will need for this endeavor. You need passion, not anger. There is a difference. You need a peaceful patience. And you need love."

"In the next fifty years," he continued, "we will see the number of Jews in the world begin to plummet like water going over Niagara Falls because of assimilation. For those of us who really care about the Jewish people it will be painful to watch and live through. If you really want to proceed, your inner joy will increase ... but it will come with a price, a painful price."

"Rabbi, I can't replace my upbringing with yours, but ..." I was unable to finish my sentence.

"Joseph, what is really at stake for you here?"

"I don't know, Rabbi. I honestly don't know."

"You must find out, Joseph. Really. It is time!"

I stopped in my tracks. At that moment, I felt completely lost.

Eden, who had been listening the whole time, said, "Really, Asher, you're like a character in melodrama. Your father and your grandfather taught you because you wanted to learn, because they were obligated to teach by those who taught them. And they taught you most by how they lived their lives. The same conditions and obligations are in place here."

I held my breath. I thought the rabbi might respond angrily. But it was amazing. He looked gently at his wife and considered. Finally, he said, "I just want to see if Joseph has what is needed if he is to go down this path."

"That is not your role here, Asher. To judge. To test. There's been too much of that mishegoss in the tradition already! The competition, hierarchies, secrets, inner circles. Share what you know! How often have you said over the years that you have no one to whom to pass on your torah, your teaching. You now have that student. Don't push him away. Don't push him away, the way my father pushed you!"

The rabbi sighed. "Now it is you who are being melodramatic," he said. But he said it without spirit. It was clear he wasn't up for a fight. And it was rather endearing to see this figure of authority, for whom my feelings fell somewhere between respect and awe, upbraided by Eden.

"Joseph, Eden is correct. We will proceed, but at some point you will need to let me know what is driving you here."

I was enormously relieved and said, perhaps a bit too quickly, "After I figure it out, I promise you'll be the first to know."

Unfortunately, I had to leave as I had told my parents that I would be home in time for us to drive to my aunt and uncle's house for the second Seder. On the way there we passed by the college where my father had studied for his B.A. He told me that despite the fact that he had gone to school after it became New Jersey law that there could be no quotas limiting the number of Jewish students at any college or university, he knew that was not always the case in the late 1940s. His girlfriend at the time had been put on the waiting list because the Jewish quota was filled. She only got to go to the college when a friend of her father's who sat on the college's Board of Trustees suggested that her father make a donation to the college. He did and she was allowed to attend, but only as a commuting student. As we continued to drive I thought about the influence of oppression on identity. I thought that it might make a good topic of discussion at the Seder, our celebration of liberation from slavery. Just before I was going to suggest that, my uncle made a comment about the whole Exodus story being a myth.

My mother then said, "There are myths that convey deep messages that are embodied by different cultures, and then there are myths that cover up lies."

"Such as what?" I asked.

"I'm glad you asked Joseph. Let's look at the myth that Jewish men don't beat their wives. Did you know that my grandfather, your great-grandfather, would beat my grandmother, your great-grandmother?" A silence then filled the room as everyone was looking at my mother. "It was my father, your Zayda, who convinced her to leave him. That was unprecedented at the beginning of the century. That is why she ended up living with us when I was growing up."

"I knew that Zayda was a tzadik," I said, using the word for a righteous person.

"Wouldn't a tzadik go to his daughter's wedding?" she said.

I was confused by her comment, but before I could react my father said, "Not now, Dear." The Seder continued, but with a cloud hanging in the air of my aunt and uncle's apartment.

On the car ride back, my mother explained that Zayda had not attended their wedding because she had gotten pregnant before she and my father got married. I pressed them with questions about the whole affair. At one point I caught my father glance at my mother as if to say Don't say any more than that. A few weeks later I would find out what they were still hiding from me.

# 13

## Religious Fanaticism

I returned to visit the rabbi the next day, still trying to assimilate what I had heard the night before, but not ready to discuss it with the rabbi. Eden suggested that we all take a walk into town.

"Where was I before you left yesterday?" asked the rabbi as we made our way up Pine Street.

"You were telling me about Einstein's early education."

"Ah, yes," said the rabbi. "As I've said, Albert's religious feeling took the form of a 'rapturous amazement at the harmony of natural law.' Abba Eban wrote something about this shortly after Albert's death: 'The Hebrew mind has been obsessed for centuries by a concept of order and harmony in the universal design. The search for laws hitherto unknown which govern cosmic forces; the doctrine of a relative harmony in nature; the idea of a calculable relationship between matter and energy—these are all more likely to emerge from a basic Hebrew philosophy and turn of mind than from many others.' So you see, even with what little Jewish upbringing he had, there were the seeds in Einstein for a great Jewish thinker!"

I was amazed at the rabbi's ability to recite quotes, word for word. It was a skill that I would later learn was part of serious Jewish study. During the period of the great Talmudic academies, tannaim functioned as walking libraries. Upon request, they would recite long passages of rabbinic wisdom, which they had memorized. And even today there are people who memorize the teachings rabbis give on Shabbas, when nothing is allowed to be written down. When Shabbas is over, they transcribe the rabbi's teaching. This ability to memorize long passages also exists in Islam: It's not unusual for a Muslim to know the entire Koran word for word.

At the corner of Pine and Nassau Streets, we turned right, heading toward the center of town. Nassau Street was alive with shoppers going in and out of stores, trucks making deliveries, and restaurants full of patrons.

"Asher," Eden said, "look in the window of Varsity Liquors. They have all these special French wines that are kosher for Passover. I want to thank him for ordering them."

"I don't know what's wrong with Manischewitz," the rabbi grumbled as Eden limped into the shop. "Never mind," he said. "In 1888, Albert entered the Luitpold Gymnasium, where he received instruction in the Jewish religion. The Proverbs of Solomon and the parts of the Jewish Bible dealing with ethics caught his interest, leaving him with a feeling for the great ethical value of the Biblical tradition. From 1892 until 1895, Albert lived with his parents in Italy, where he studied the Psalms, Talmud, and other aspects of Jewish history. His father became concerned that Albert was not getting the proper skills he would need for employment and decided to send Albert to the Swiss Federal Polytechnic School in Zurich, but Albert failed the entrance exam. The Polytechnic's principal saw that there was more to this teenager than the tests showed, however, and suggested that Albert be sent to a canton school in Aarau, Switzerland, for a year."

Eden emerged from the store and we continued our walk. "Albert already had great, deep thoughts. In Switzerland, he wrote an essay, which he sent to one of his uncles, titled "Concerning the Investigation of Ether in Magnetic Fields." By the age of sixteen, some of the groundwork had been laid that would eventually lead ten years later to his discovery of the Special Theory of Relativity in 1905!"

We came to Washington Road, made a left, and headed down to Carnegie Lake, passing near the Princeton University Chapel. Farther down the hill, we could see Palmer Stadium and Jadwin Gym. We reached the boathouse on the lake where the crew teams kept their shells and sat on a bench facing the water. "Einstein had the same kind of young precocious mind as Abraham," said the rabbi. "Maimonides writes ..." The rabbi closed his eyes and recited: "'After Abraham was weaned, while still an infant, his mind began to reflect. By day and by night he was thinking and wondering: How is it possible that this celestial sphere should continuously be guiding the world and have no one to guide it and cause it to turn round; for it cannot be that it turns round of itself ... Abraham had no teacher, no one to instruct him, but his mind was busily working and reflecting until he had attained the way of truth, apprehended the correct line of thought, and knew that there is one God, and that God guides the celestial sphere and created everything ...'

"Albert's early interest in religious questions was tempered by an aversion toward religious institutions. He witnessed those who were forced to go to religious services and compared them with young men who are forced into military service against their will. By age sixteen, Albert had rejected both rigid militaristic Germany and organized religious Judaism. And let's be honest, Joseph: All religions can become fanatic. If we understand that God is the ultimate power in the universe, and if we think we know what God wants, it can become intoxicating. There is a danger in all religions for that feeling of absolute power to become pervasive and corrupting."

The rabbi stopped speaking and we looked out at the water, lightly ruffled by wind, shimmering in the sun. I thought about all the wars that had been fought in the name of God. "Rabbi, this has only been reinforced by my class in politics; religion has been the source of so much misery and suffering over the years. In many ways religion is no better than secular governments or philosophies. So why should we turn to it for guidance?" I asked.

I saw a flame kindle in the rabbi's eyes. "Let me give you a teaching," he said.

"Do you know the story of the Akeida, the binding of Isaac?" the rabbi asked.

"Where God asks Abraham to sacrifice his son?" I was surprised. "I have always thought that story illustrates an absolute adherence to faith," I said. "Exactly the opposite of what we're talking about!"

"True," said the rabbi. "The Akeida is traditionally read as the ultimate test of Abraham's faith. The classic reading is that Abraham is considered to have passed the test, since he was willing to follow God's command to sacrifice Isaac. But there are other ways to read the text, including one that is truly astounding. Do you remember that Abraham and Isaac walked up the mountain together?"

"Yes," I said.

"In Hebrew that is 'vayelchoo shneyhem yachdav.' But after the incident Abraham returns alone—'vayashav avraham el n'arav'—to the servants." The rabbi paused. "So, Joseph," he said, "how would you understand the text?"

I felt an intense excitement at the question. I had read the story but never pondered its subtleties, and suddenly I felt a world, and a tradition, opening up inside me. "Isaac was so shaken by the experience that he wanted to be left alone," I said. "Or he didn't trust his father after what had happened, and so did not walk back down the mountain with him."

"Nice readings," said the rabbi. "But I said something astounding."

"Abraham really killed him." I said the most shocking thing that I could think of, although I couldn't believe any reader would interpret the story this way.

"Excellent. And let's say that's the case, what would you then have to deal with?"

"Well, Isaac hasn't married yet, which we know he does. So how could a dead person get married and have children?"

"How could he?" asked the rabbi.

"I'm stumped."

"Don't think so Jewish."

"He was resurrected," I offered, again not believing what I was saying.

"Sounds too Christian, doesn't it?"

"Yes."

"But in Second Kings Chapter Four we read that the prophet Elisha brought a child back from the dead. Perhaps the angel arrived too late to stay Abraham's knife. Perhaps he did kill his son! This reading of the text was a way of saying that the sacrifice of Isaac was on par with that of Jesus—an outlook that gained popularity with Jews during the Middle Ages when Jews were being slaughtered by Christians."

"Jews believed this?"

"Some did."

"I find it hard to accept."

"I understand that. Let's look at another way to understand the whole episode. Yes, Abraham passes a test. Kierkegaard wrestled with this incident in his work Fear and Trembling. He said that 'The story of Abraham contains a teleological suspension of the ethical'; in other words, we're dealing here with something beyond ethical norms. Kierkegaard puzzled over what struck him as the absurd notion that a father, by killing his son, would please God."

"I once had a conversation with Albert about this. When he first got here, the Institute for Advanced Studies was housed in Fine Hall, now called Jones Hall, on the Princeton campus. Across the fireplace in the common room was carved Einstein's famous quote in German, Raffiniert ist der Herr-Gott, aber boshaft ist er nicht, The Lord is subtle, but he is not malicious."

"I like that, Rabbi," I said.

The rabbi smiled at me and continued. "Albert and I were having tea, his ever-present pipe filled the air, and the subject of the Akeida came up. I said to him that in my eyes the test was not that Abraham was willing to offer up Isaac in sacrifice—to kill in the name of God. No! It is that even when Abraham was in that moment of zealous fervor, when the knife was raised above his head ready to do God's will, he was still able to hear the angel say, 'This is not what God wants, there is another way.' Let's listen to the text."

The rabbi recited in melodious Hebrew: "'Vayikra elav malach adonoi min hashamayim vayomer avraham avraham.—Then the angel of the Lord called to him from heaven: Abraham! Abraham!' This word vayikra: It means 'And He called,' or, in most cases, 'And God called.' Joseph, do you think God still calls to us?"

"I would like to think so, but I don't know how," I said. I shrugged my shoulders.

"Yes, it is often hard to hear that call. But one way is

through the word itself, 'vayikra.' In the Talmud the word 'kra' which is the root of 'vayikra' is also a word for the Torah. That is to say that God continues to call out to us by our ongoing engagement with the Book, its language and content, what is written and what is not. Can you feel the resonance?"

I nodded and, indeed, it was as if something inside me was on fire. It was so beautiful! Abraham could still hear the angel's voice.

"Where does the angel call from?" the rabbi asked.

"Heaven."

"Why?"

"The angel didn't have time to get to earth and tell Abraham to stop."

"Exactly, the angel's call is a call across the universe—and its echo is still with us today. All religions have that angelic voice— a counter to religious fanaticism and blindness. The cultivation of the individual's ability to hear that voice is one of the great challenges of all religions—perhaps the greatest challenge. We must not allow religion to be hijacked by extremists."

The rabbi paused for a moment and took a deep breath. Eden put her hand over his and patted it gently. "Albert did not reject Judaism," the rabbi continued. "What he rejected was Orthodox Judaism, which conforms to standardized, set-down doctrines and practices and sees those who understand things differently as wrong—as the very word Orthodox implies. Ortho means correct; dox, opinion or thought. Albert knew how misguided this is. He once said to me, 'Actually, it is a very difficult thing to even define a Jew. The closest that I can come to describing it is to ask you to visualize a snail. A snail that you see at the ocean consists of the body that is snuggled inside of the house which it always carries around with it. But let's picture what would happen if we lifted the shell off of the snail. Would we not still describe the unprotected body as a snail? In just the same way, a Jew who sheds his faith along the way, or who even picks up a different one, is still a Jew.'"

"That's a pretty graphic image!"

"It is! But Einstein's Judaism was much more complex than a snail that sheds its shell. His 'Hebraic' mind sought to understand how God created the universe. He allowed himself to be awed by the mystery of it all—that which could not be explained. His Judaism— his deep sense of ethics, his rejection of fanaticism of all sorts, his deep pacifistic beliefs—is how he heard that angelic voice, which has been echoing across the universe since the dawn of human consciousness.

"For Albert, religion was a much deeper process than thinking the correct way. For Albert, a better adjective would be a Paradoxical Jew. 'Para' meaning 'beyond,' so that paradoxical means 'beyond thought or opinion.' While we have seen that Albert wished to understand how God created the universe, we also know that he was awed by the mystery of it all—that which could not be explained."

"Rabbi," I said, "mystery seemed to play a big part in Einstein's relationship to Judaism. I remember my grandfather once telling me that when Einstein was asked about his belief in God he said 'I bow to the Unknown.'"

"Yes Joseph, you are absolutely correct. I once had a very interesting conversation with Albert about this one spring," he replied. "This time of year the Jewish calendar reminds us of the centrality, the mystery, and the unknown through the holidays of Purim and Passover. There is an interesting connection between these two holidays. In addition to the custom of giving to the poor, mattanot le-evyonim, on Purim, there is also the custom of giving gifts of food to friends, mishloach manot. One year we decided to give some food to Albert, his sister Maja, his stepdaughter Margot from his second wife Elsa, and his secretary Helen Dukas, who all lived together in the house on Mercer Street. For years that quartet lived there."

"At one point during that visit, Albert commented on how he thought many of the customs around the holidays and even some of the holidays themselves were quaint anachronisms. I told him that Purim celebrates, among a number of things, the hiddeness, the mystery of life. I explained to him that on Purim we wear masks that hide our faces. He responded that that was not a custom unique to Judaism. He noted that many cultures have such days in their calendars—Halloween and Mardi Gras to name two. I then reminded him that Esther, who is the hero of the holiday, has a name that literally means, 'hidden,' as she originally hides her Jewish identity from the King. I also told him that God is completely hidden from this Biblical story, never making an appearance or even being mentioned in its pages. That got his attention. I also said to him that in much of the world; the ground is hidden, covered by winter's snow.

"I told him that with Passover we find a transition as we start the Seder by hiding a piece of Matzoh, the Affikoman, which is then found, discovered, revealed by the end of the meal. 'Albert,' I said to him, 'that is what you have been doing all your life, looking for God's Affikoman.' He laughed. 'Freedom,' I continued to say, 'is both the celebration of discovery and self-discovery, but freedom without direction can become a meaningless wandering. So, for example, that is why we count the days between Passover and Shavuot.'"

The rabbi turned to me and said, "We started to do that last night at the second Seder, with the counting of the Omer, the time between the barley harvest and the wheat harvest.

"And what does the holiday of Shavuot celebrate?" he asked me.

80

"The revelation of the Torah at Mount Sinai," I answered without losing a beat.

"Good," said the Rabbi. "And what is the equivalent American holiday to Passover?"

"The Fourth of July."

"Okay. And what would the equivalent of Shavuot be?"

I paused and thought, and thought some more, and finally looked at him with an expression that said I did not know.

"Don't feel so bad," he said. "Most people don't get it either. Constitution Day is September 17th. So on July 4th we celebrate our freedom, while on September 17th we celebrate the rights and responsibilities that go with those freedoms. It is interesting that in our Jewish tradition we count the days between our holiday of Freedom, and our Constitution, the Torah. Its message is that there needs to be a connection between the two, for freedom without the rights and responsibilities that go with it can lead to anarchy. We here in America love to celebrate our freedoms, which we should, but we celebrate less the responsibilities that go along with our freedoms. Also is that freedom used to refine and elevate our lives and our souls, or does it become the license for that which is shallow and empty, devoid of deep meaning?"

"That sounds fine, but who is to say what is meaningful and what is shallow? Who gets to arbitrate and decide?"

"Ideally, the individual and not the state. Since the turn of the century, we have witnessed those who can't deal with the weight of such a decision. These are people who feel more comfortable when life is presented as black and white. They are insecure and uncomfortable with the responsibilities of freedom and so create systems that tell them, and they hope us as well, what to think, what to wear, and how to live our lives with no digression from the rules."

"Liberal Western democracies, as imperfect as they may be,

are the best system we have come up with when it comes to creating a means to allow humans to develop to their fullest potential. As Churchill reminds us, 'Democracy is the worst form of government except for all those others that have been tried.' The system is not perfect, and can sometimes lead people to be more concerned with their freedoms in a way that can border on the decadent. As it is a human creation and therefore, imperfect, the system needs to view freedom with an understanding of the gray areas of life."

We rose and continued our walk in silence for a time, enjoying the warm afternoon breeze that was picking up and blowing the water of the lake into waves, which lapped against the shore. Sailboats were cutting along through the small chop.

"Oh, how Albert loved to sail," said the rabbi. There was sadness in his voice.

"You miss him, Dear, don't you?" said Eden.

"I do," said the rabbi. "It was a privilege to be in his company. And I miss our conversations. I miss his deep commitment to the spirit of tolerance for differences in the world. As a scientist, he knew that the more diversity there is in nature, the healthier it is— and that the same holds true for people. We need a multitude of religions, languages, and cultures. I miss his wild hair and baggy pants which he refused to hold up with suspenders. And I miss his distrust of dogma and authority—his defiant non-conformity. How he hated religious fanaticism! He knew it was, perhaps, the most lethal of the forms of totalitarian thought that have plagued humanity. We once talked about this need for diversity in regards to the Tower of Babel. Albert said that he had always been puzzled by the message, the interpretation of the text that God had punished humans by creating different languages, each incomprehensible to the other."

"That's what I've always thought, too, and wondered why God is always punishing people?"

"Yes, God punishes at times, but never for the sake of punishment, but rather to teach. In this case it was not a punishment, but a gift."

"A gift? How can a punishment be a gift?"

"Listen closely," said the rabbi, "and a new interpretation appears. After the flood we learn, according to the text, that the nations of the earth had branched out with their own languages. And then we read at the beginning of the episode of the Tower of Babel that the world was of one language and the same words. Not only were they of one language, but they were even limited in the words that they used. This means that they were limited in their range of thought and expression. When I said this to Albert he cocked his head, and I knew then that I had his full attention. The Israeli philosopher and scientist Yeshayahu Leibowitz teaches that the building of the city and the Tower represents 'the concentration of all of mankind about a single topic—where there will not be difference of opinion and there will not be a struggle over different viewpoints and over different values.' Leibowitz understands that the story is about totalitarian rule, the form of government that caused Einstein to flee Germany and come here. Totalitarianism despises individualism. It wants everyone to dress alike, look alike, speak alike, and think alike. It crushes the human spirit and causes whole cultures to become barbarous, with no regard for human life. We find this description of culture in a Midrash on the building of the Tower of Babel. The Midrash, written fifteen hundred years ago, says that if a human fell off the Tower no one cared, but if a brick fell there was an outcry of loss. That was the regime of Babel.

"I asked Einstein if he thought that kind of regime should be punished or changed. He said, yes, such a regime was unhealthy and unjust and should change. And that is just what happens in the story, he added. God confuses the people of Babel's speech into many languages so they all sound like they are babbling to one another. Is that a punishment?"

"Isn't it?" I said.

"Leibowitz offers a different reading. He argues, and I think he's right, that the mixing up of languages isn't punitive— rather it's correction back to how things were supposed to be, a gift for us reminding us to be more human; that one of the most important elements of humanity is our diversity. After the first failing of humanity ..."

"What was that?" I interrupted.

"'The earth was filled with lawlessness ... All flesh had corrupted its ways on earth,' Genesis 6," the rabbi answered. "At any rate, after that, God brought down the flood. Right after the waters had receded and humanity had reconstituted itself, we failed again! This time, rather than wipe out the world, God makes a correction in the plan that addresses a specific flaw."

"A flaw in God's plan?"

The rabbi smiled. "A thread runs through the end of the stories of both the Flood and the Tower of Babel. After the Flood, God puts a rainbow in the sky as a reminder that he will never again destroy the world through water. And what causes a rainbow? A ray of light refracted though water. Out of the one comes the many, which is both a theological and scientific statement. So at the end of the Tower of Babel story the use of many languages is restored. Genesis reminds us of the importance of diversity over and over. Remember during the beginning of creation as God creates each thing in the universe, God calls it 'good.' Albert, who usually had something to say, was unusually quiet and pensive after I had shared this teaching with him.

"Pardon for this digression, but having lived through what I have witnessed in my lifetime this century, I think one of the greatest challenges the human race faces is to learn how to build a world and societies that celebrate diversity." The rabbi paused, seemingly lost in thought. I was curious. Was the rabbi referring to something in his past? Did all of his family manage to get out of Europe before World War II? Perhaps some of them had been murdered in the camps?

My curiosity got the better of me. "What do you mean?" I asked.

He waved his hand in a dismissive motion.

"He stole me away from my father," said Eden; the mischief, which was never far from the surface, bubbling up.

The rabbi shushed her.

"No," she said. "Joseph has a right to know. He needs to know—for his own journey." And before he could say a word, she continued. "Asher was the star student of my father, Rabbi Yehuda Ramot, a gifted disciple of the Netziv of Volozhin," she said in her wry way. "But Asher broke away from my father, who had been one of his tutors, and went to study with Rabbi Mordecai Kaplan. You know who he is, Joseph?"

"I'm afraid not."

"Doesn't matter," she said. "You will. Kaplan was the founder of Reconstructionism. Kaplan's father had also studied with this same Netziv. But Kaplan too broke from Orthodox Judaism. By that time, Asher and I were already in love, and I had to choose— Asher or my father. I chose Asher."

She stopped speaking and looked at the rabbi, but he remained quiet. "Go on, tell him, Asher," she prodded.

He sighed. "All right," he said with a shrug. "I know by now that it is my wife who knows what is good for me. I went to ask my future shver, father-in-law, for his blessing. 'You are an epikuros, a heretic—you do not exist for me,' he said. 'When you are ready to come back and acknowledge that you have strayed from derekh, the path that I showed you, then we will talk. Until then I will see that you are put in herem. I will see that you are excommunicated within our community—no one will be able to sit within four amot (feet) of you, or speak to you from less than that distance, or break bread with you, or count you towards a minyan.' But I could not abide by that kind of closed-minded orthodoxy that shuts out the world. That is so firmly convinced by its rightness. That thinks it has a                    l                                        l the answers."

"I'm sorry," I said, looking for something to say. I was overwhelmed that they were confiding in me in this way, and wondering, with all that, what Eden meant about my own journey.

"You, too, will make choices," said Eden. "I hope your choices will not be as painful as ours. Nonetheless, you will have to choose."

As she said that, I thought of Corina and Billy and wondered if I was making the right choices.

"Let's get back to Einstein," said the rabbi. "I want to tell Joseph how Albert came to realize just how Jewish he was."

I was both relieved and, I confess, a bit disappointed with the shift in conversation.

"We were talking about the centrality of mystery and the unveiling of that which is hidden," said the rabbi. "It was in Prague where Albert's Judaism was unmasked."

"Wasn't Kafka from Prague?" I asked. "I studied him last semester."

Suddenly, I saw the rabbi turn pale. "Yes, Joseph, he was, and he and Einstein knew each other. But please forgive me if we stop here for now. Let's walk back toward our house. I must confess that I'm feeling very tired."

"Are you sure you can walk, my darling?" Eden said.

"Yes, but slowly."

We retraced our steps. I hoped to come back the next day, but Eden said that the rabbi needed to rest and that I should let them know when I would be back again. I was intrigued by the notion of Einstein and Kafka together and I did not want to wait so long. I returned to Vermont and decided to return two weeks later. In the meantime the mention of Kafka influenced my dreams. As the goat fell in sacrifice, I could hear voices in the Temple courtyard murmuring in confusion, a line from one of Kafka's works, "The Messiah will only arrive when we no longer need him."

# 14

## Choices

I could not shake Eden's comment about the choices I would face, and Kafka's entrance into my dreams created an unsettling effect. I had not told my parents or the rabbi about moving out of my dorm room. One morning I showed up at the Counseling Center of the University of Vermont hoping to speak to someone. I had not made an appointment. Fortunately one of the counselors had an opening.

She offered me a glass of orange juice. I told her about my fight with Billy, and how I had first gone to Corina's apartment but when I stood outside her door I heard another man's voice, and so I had found a room off-campus. But my money was running out to cover the rent.

She asked me if I had thought about leaving the apartment and moving back in with Billy. I told her I wasn't sure, adding, "You're supposed to tell me what to do."

"I am?"

"Yeah, people come here and you tell them what to do so their lives are all better."

"Joseph, not exactly. I try to help you find out what you need to do, but I don't tell you what to do."

"I knew I should have gone to see the Chabad rabbi," I mumbled under my breath.

"And what would he have done for you?"

"He would have told me what to do."

"You sound pretty sure of that, but you came here instead, Joseph, didn't you?"

I looked up at her, my eyes welling up in tears, "I don't know what I'm becoming."

"Joseph, the fact that you came to the Counseling Center and not to the Chabad rabbi speaks louder than words. You have already chosen."

We talked some more and I agreed that I would move back to my dorm room.

"But I still have this pull," I said to her.

"Joseph, do you really think that living a religious life is about cutting yourself off from the world?"

"Monks do."

"Joseph, you don't really want to become a monk. What you want to do is run away from the inner struggle that you are engaged in. This is a very important process that you are going through. Your challenge, and there lies the tension, is how to weave the life you have now with the life that you want. Remember, as with musical instruments, it is the tension in the strings that is the source that enables the music to be heard."

Later that week I had another conversation. It was with Dr. Ackberg, my political science teacher. It was not the conversation that I wanted to hear.

"Joseph," he started, "You had the potential to be one of my best students, and then you got religion. Sometimes I think that you and others who seek out religion are unsettled by a world that can't be counted on and figured out. Even Einstein had trouble with that concept and wasted the last thirty years of his life looking for a unified field theory.

"Last semester you took my Introduction to Problems of Political Thought class. It was clear to me from the start by the questions you asked that you had what it took to understand the mechanisms of politics. You knew how impressed I was by your insights and grasp of the material, so I invited you to attend my upper-level seminar this semester, even though you were still a freshman. After all those years of teaching I thought I had found my protégé."

His words hit me like a ton of bricks. I thought the rabbi was to be my mentor. How blind had I become? I was so wrapped up in my spiritual journey that I had forgotten about my interest in pursuing a political career. Before I even had time to process that thought he continued.

"It was subtle at first, Joseph, and then became more and more apparent. Your questions became less sharp, and then I could tell you were doing less and less of the readings, seeming to daydream in class, then I noticed you started to cover your head. And then you started wearing strings that hung from your waist. You are like a deer caught in headlights—trapped. When I ask you what is going on, you seem evasive, as though you don't want to speak or you are not sure what to say."

Arrogance can be the cover for uncertainty and inner confusion, so I shot back. "How is the world any better for politicians? What have they brought upon the world all these centuries, nothing but war and misery? And it's all part of the same larger picture of capitalism and power. John Maynard Keynes had it right when he said, 'Capitalism is the extraordinary belief that the nastiest of men, for the nastiest of reasons, will somehow work for the benefit of us all.' And then there were all those misguided Jewish socialists of the last century. They took God out of Messianism and gave us totalitarian communism. I still have a political cartoon that appeared a few years ago in the newspaper. It was a drawing of the Great Seal of the United States with the caption, 'What is the goal of American foreign policy? To make the world safe for hypocrisy.' We believe in democracy but we support despots and dictators all over the world. The Shah of Iran is just one example. Someday he will be replaced and will the Iranians then still be our friends for having supported his secret police so long!? As the Arab proverb goes, 'The enemy of my enemy is my friend,' and that has been the guiding light for too much of history."

Before I finished with my next breath he interjected. "Joseph, a nice overview pointing out some serious flaws in business as usual, but what in your moral indignation would you replace it with?"

"With the wisdom of those who look at the world as a place to raise the holy sparks that have been trampled down by the greed of ego, power, and money."

"Well, if that is not a whole lot of crap. Holy sparks! Are you really telling me that religion does not suffer from ego, power, and money? Joseph, I don't know what is happening to you. Why do you think I have been teaching all of these years? Hoping that someone, just one person, might come along and learn from all this folly and try to turn things around. For a while there I thought it might be you. That one student of mine would come along, and with the skills and the knowledge who I could teach, and who would then go out there and rock the boat. But I can see I was wrong, it's not you."

# 15

## Prague and Kafka

I returned home shortly afterwards. At breakfast, as the smell of bacon and eggs filled the kitchen, my parents asked if I wanted to go to a matinee showing of Woody Allen's Annie Hall, which had just been released.

"I've already made plans to see the rabbi," I said.

"Your grandfather," my mother said, a sardonic edge in her voice, "would be so happy to hear that you chose visiting a rabbi over going to a movie. You've been spending quite a bit of time with this person. I hope he isn't brainwashing you."

"What do you mean?" I asked.

"We don't want to lose you," said my father.

"That's funny. You don't mind hearing the latest torah from Rabbi Woody Allen, your favorite rabbi," I said under my breath.

"What did you just say?" my mother asked, raising her voice.

I couldn't believe that they had heard me. I also could not believe what I had said. I never would have said something like that before I had met the rabbi. My heart raced as I felt my choices at that moment: confrontation or placation. I chose the latter, making a lighthearted comment about how rabbis come in all shapes and sizes. But I knew that next time such a diversion would not work.

I pondered what had happened as I arrived at the rabbi's in the early afternoon. I found him and Eden sitting on the front porch, with the living room windows open, listening to classical music.

"Joseph, do you recognize this piece of music?" he asked.

"Rabbi, I'm not sure but it sounds like Hatikva, Israel's national anthem."

"Yes! We are listening to Smetana's The Moldau, the river that flows through Prague. The E minor melody that you just heard was based on an Eastern European folk tune that he included in his symphony. This recording of the piece includes a local Princeton musician, who we knew and who grew up on Mercer Street next door to Albert. She said that she became a professional musician because of her success at mathematics—and that she attributed to Albert.

"She once told us that she had trouble with her arithmetic homework when she was ten years old. She had heard that at number 112 Mercer there lived a big mathematician, who was also a very good man. She knew that he was a good man since some of her friends had gone trick-or-treating at his house and he played the violin for them! So she grabbed some homemade fudge and went and knocked on his door and asked him to help her with her homework. He was very willing, but with a chuckle accused her of trying to bribe him with the chocolate. She said that he explained everything very well and that it was easier to understand than when her teacher explained it in school. He said that she should come whenever she found a problem too difficult. When her mother heard what she had done, she went over to apologize to Albert. He said: 'You don't have to excuse yourself. I have certainly learned more from the conversations with the child than she did from me.'"

We all laughed.

"At any rate," the rabbi continued, "the river flowing through Prague actually has two names, "Molded" in German and "Vltava" in Czech. The two names represent the people of her banks who were split in two: the Czech and German populations of Bohemia."

Eden interjected, "According to Jewish legend, in the sixteenth century Rabbi Yehudah Loew recited secret incantations over mud from of that river to fashion the Golem, a Jewish version of Frankenstein, to save the Jews from persecution."

I then said, looking for something to add, "And every baseball used in the major leagues is rubbed with mud from the Delaware River, and only ten people know where it comes from."

"Are we finished?" said the rabbi with a bit of both exasperation and humor in his voice. He then continued, "Albert found himself caught up in that division when he accepted a teaching position at the German University of Prague in 1911. The university was fraught with the growing tension between the German and Czech populations of the city. In 1888, the Austro-Hungarian Emperor split the university in two: one half German, the other Czech."

"That's ironic," I said, "I know that Einstein renounced his German citizenship when he was a teenager."

"It was more than that," said the rabbi. "He had to take out Austro-Hungarian citizenship to join the faculty. If questions of nationality were thrust upon him, so were questions of religious identity. When it came to filling out 'religion' on his application, he put down 'none.' But Emperor Franz Josef, who personally signed the faculty appointments, would not appoint anyone who did not state their religion. Reluctantly, Albert had the form changed to read 'Mosaic,' the term for someone Jewish, so he could get the appointment."

"I thought that Einstein always saw himself as a Jew," I said "Why would he be reluctant to acknowledge that he was 'Jewish' on the form?"

The rabbi sighed. "Filling out a form pressed all his buttons," he said. "What Albert had rejected was Judaism as an organized religion. The Austrian physicist Phillip Frank said he and Albert were once at a police station in Prague to get a passport. A Jewish man asked Einstein if he knew a restaurant in Prague where the food was strictly kosher. Einstein mentioned the name of a hotel that was known to be kosher. The man then asked Einstein if the 'hotel [was] really strictly kosher?' This annoyed Einstein. 'Actually, only an ox eats strictly kosher,' he replied. The pious man was hurt and looked indignantly at Einstein. Einstein, however, explained that his statement was not offensive at all, but quite objective and innocent: 'An ox eats grass, and this is the only strictly kosher food because nothing has been done to it.'

"Was Einstein right, Rabbi?" I asked. I had only the foggiest notions of the laws of kashrut.

"Honestly, I don't think that Albert understood kashrut. It is a spiritual discipline, as well as the awareness that when we eat meat, we are taking a life. That is another discussion for another time. The incident illustrates Albert's disdain for the rigidity and artifice of religion.

"But there was more to why he was reluctant to openly identify as Jewish, and that had to do with the development of his own Jewish identity. Years later, when he was in a similar situation, he did not even think twice about declaring himself 'Jewish' on a form. As I mentioned to you previously, there was a maturation of his Jewish identity as the years went on."

"Interesting," I said, as I shifted in my rocking chair, finding myself thinking again about my own Judaism.

Looking straight at me, the rabbi said, "Everyone has their own path. They find their own way. The maturation of which I speak is common to us all and exists in all religions. That same dynamic operates in your life. Joseph, you have given me hints of a desire to be more Jewish. A part of you is waiting for the rest of you to catch up to integrate the who you are now with the who you want to be. With Albert, I am not sure that it was the same process, but he clearly had the foundations of his Judaism in place. When the conditions were right, that identity asserted itself. The difference between you and Albert is that it was external anti-Semitism that forced him to identify as a Jew, while, for you, I believe, it is much more of an internal process."

"How can I help that process happen, Rabbi?"

"First of all, as I learned, spiritual development is a process. It is never complete. You never 'get there,' and it is life-long. Our system of Torah reading reminds us of this lesson. We start on Simchat Torah, right after the fall harvest holiday of Sukkot, with the beginning of Sefer Beresheet, the Book of Genesis and the story of the creation of the universe. We take a whole year to read through the Five Books of Moses and end up at the end of Sefer Dvarim, the Book of Deuteronomy, with Moses and the Children of Israel looking across the Jordan River into the Promised Land. Now, the tradition could have ended with the first chapter of the Book of Joshua, when we read about our entry into the land of Israel. But instead the Torah ends there, and we roll the scrolls back again to the beginning of

Creation and start all over.

"The point here is that it is the journey, not reaching the final destination, that is most important. Even if you 'reach' a destination, you are not the same existential 'you' who began the journey. All that has happened along the way has changed you. So in a certain sense 'you,' the existential person you are now, will never 'get there,' because you will be a different 'you' when you arrive."

I thought for a moment about what the rabbi had just said. Then I said, "Rabbi, I came here because I wanted to find out how Einstein could help me with my own feelings of confusion and a yearning that I've had since I was very young."

"I hope you don't entirely model yourself on Albert," said Eden. "He may have been the smartest man in the world, but he was incredibly absentminded. More than once, I was in the deli off Witherspoon Street when the owner took a call from Helen Dukas, who let him know that Albert was walking over. A few minutes later, in would walk Albert with a list pinned to his jacket. Once his order was filled, the total would go on his tab since he was not good at keeping track of money. Then the deli owner would call his home and let them know that Albert was on his way. During World War I, Albert was delayed crossing the border from Germany into Switzerland because he could not remember his name. It's not surprising that one of his school teachers said that his mind was like a sieve."

While the day was warm enough to sit outside, it had been cloudy, and the sky was growing increasingly dark. Finally it began to rain. A real spring downpour, accompanied by thunder and lightning.

"Shouldn't we go inside?" I asked.

"This is one of our favorite pastimes," said Eden, "sitting on the porch during a storm." With the sound of thunder, the rabbi and

Eden recited, "Baruch atah adonay eloheynu melech ha'olam sheko-cho ugvurato maley olam" translating for me, "Blessed are You, Ruler of the Universe whose power and might fill the world." We took in the power, sounds, and smell of the storm. When the wind began to push the rain onto the porch, we headed inside.

The rabbi and I sat in the living room so we could still hear the storm through the open window. Eden turned off the music and went to read in the dining room.

"Prague, like many of the great European cities," the rabbi said, "had an important intellectual life in its cafés and salons. Café Slavia was the leading Czech café, a favorite spot for Czech writers, journalists, and progressive thinkers. Albert would go there and to Café Louvre to talk to colleagues or scribble equations on pieces of paper. Nearby, at the Café Arco, was another intellectual circle that included the young and still unknown writer Franz Kafka."

"Finally," I said, "Kafka and Einstein. I've been waiting to hear about this."

"Yes, it's interesting," said the rabbi. "But first you need to understand a bit about Prague in the second decade of the twentieth century. The richness and depth of Prague's intellectual life during those years included, at different times, such writers as Rainer Maria Rilke, Martin Buber, and Thomas Mann. Second, although about half of the Germans there were Jews, the relation of the Jews to the other Germans assumed a problematic character because the racial theories, later to become Nazi creed, had already begun to influence the Sudeten Germans. On the one hand, the Germans wanted the Jews as allies against the Czechs. On the other hand, they did not want to identify themselves too closely with the Jews.

"Only ten years earlier, a Jewish cobbler, Leopold Hilsner, had been falsely accused of performing a ritual murder on a young Christian woman near the town of Polna, about seventy miles southeast of Prague, and sentenced to death for the crime. His case became a cause célèbre in Eastern Europe as well as a manifestation of growing anti-Semitism. In the same way that Emile Zola had come to the defense of Dreyfus in France in the last decade of the nineteenth century, Tomas Masaryk, at the time a young member of the Austro-Hungarian Parliament and the future President of the Czech Republic, accomplished the same for Hilsner in getting his death sentence commuted. However, he was immediately tried again for another murder, also on trumped-up charges because he was Jewish, and sentenced to death. The sentence was commuted to life imprisonment and Hilsner was finally pardoned in 1918 near the end of World War I.

"Finally, the Anarchist movement and political assassination of the late nineteenth and early twentieth century was still hauntingly alive in the 1920s. Anarchists had assassinated the French president, Sadi Carnot, in 1894; Elizabeth of Austria, the wife of Franz Joseph I of Austria in 1898; King Umberto I of Italy in 1900; and President William McKinley in 1901. And in June 1914 Archduke Franz Ferdinand, the heir to the Austro-Hungarian Empire, and his wife, Sophie, would be assassinated by a Slavic nationalist. This assassination set in motion the events that lead to World War I and many of the subsequent political events of the twentieth century.

"Kafka and Einstein were part of a dynamic salon that met at the home of Berta Fanta on Tuesday evenings in her apartment on the historic Wenceslas Square in the center of Prague, not far from the Jewish quarter. Decades later, in Princeton, Berta's daughter-in-law, Johanna Fantova, who I have already mentioned to you, became Albert's companion during the last part of his life. Fanta's was one of Prague's eminent intellectual circles and included the physicist Phillip Frank, the philosophers Christian von Ehrenfel and Felix

Weltsch, Rudolph Steiner, the father of anthroposophy, Fanta's son-in-law Hugo Bergman, and Max Brod, who published Kafka's writings. Brod also wrote a novel, The Redemption of Tycho Brahe, in which the character of Kepler is modeled on Einstein."

"How was Einstein portrayed?" I asked.

"That's a good question. Fanta was an ardent Zionist, as were Brod and Weltsch, and Brod's portrayal of the fictional Kepler was a veiled criticism of Einstein's lack of enthusiasm for Zionism, which would change, by the way, a few years later, when Albert was appointed professor at the University of Berlin. In Prague, Einstein could not be bothered with such matters. He was immersed in work on the idea of light bending through gravity, which would eventually lead to his General Theory of Relativity."

"It must have been an exciting time," I said.

"While Kafka and Albert were part of a mostly Jewish circle," the rabbi continued, "their connection to Judaism was minimal." The rabbi walked down the hall to his study and returned with a book. "In his famous Letter to His Father, Kafka wrote about attending services at the Pinchas Synagogue, his family's shul: 'And so I yawned and dozed through the many hours and did my best to enjoy the few little bits of variety there were, as for instance when the Ark of the Covenant was opened, which always reminded me of the shooting galleries where a cupboard door would open in the same way whenever one hit a bull's-eye.'"

"That's pretty funny, but Rabbi," I paused for a brief moment, "services can be very boring."

"Well, they can be, but that is another discussion."

"Joseph, don't let him stall you on important questions like that," said Eden as she went by to get the mail that had just arrived.

The rabbi looked at her, smiled, and then said without missing a beat, "Joseph, all spiritual disciplines have a repetitive element in them that, yes, can be boring at times, but is also the key to why they work. In part that repetitiveness provides an anchor, a constant, in our lives; as so much in our lives can change, we seek—we need—a grounding that we can count on to be there. Breathing is repetitive, our heart beating is repetitive, the earth circles the sun, and the moon circles the earth. Repetition is a key to how the world operates that we often lose sight of in the hustle and bustle of our lives."

The rabbi then returned the conversation to Einstein and Kafka. "Kafka's relationship to Judaism, like Einstein's, kept developing. Kafka's friendship with the actor Jizchak Lowey, who was performing in the Yiddish theater company in Prague, had a positive influence on his Jewish identity."

"It's hard for me to think that so many of the great writers and thinkers who were Jewish had such an ambivalent relationship to their Judaism."

"Remember what Albert said about a snail still being a snail. Everyone develops in his or her own way. Our task—my task, I should say—is to help people in their journey; to awaken their souls to the beauty and wisdom of our tradition."

The rabbi's initial inclusion of me in this task made me feel good. He continued, "In truth Einstein and Kafka in Prague were a study in contrasts. While Kafka was quiet at Fanta's salon, Einstein joined in discussions. Albert was already well known; Kafka, unknown. Both were obsessed with the chaos of the world and the universe—chaos reflected in the paintings of Picasso and Cubists. Kafka embraced and entered the madness of that chaos, while Albert tried to find order in it. Albert once said to me about Kafka's The Castle, that he 'couldn't read it because of its perversity.'"

"Asher," Eden called out. "You need to take your nap."

"Joseph, I usually nap for only an hour. Feel free to wait for me here in the living room or in my study."

"I don't want to impose on you," I said.

"Your visits are no imposition at all. Besides, Berlin is the next crucial stage in Einstein's Jewish development, and I'd like to share it with you soon after telling you about his Prague experience."

The rabbi went upstairs, and I went over to his study. I had seen it only partially through the door in the dining room. It felt sacrosanct, and I had not asked to enter it. I took a deep breath and walked in. The walls were lined with bookshelves that were filled with books from floor to ceiling. On the wall to the left as one entered were six tall filing cabinets. A large desk, piled with books and papers, faced a big bay window. The photo of Michelangelo's David hung next to the desk.

I walked over to the bookshelves and scanned the titles. The books were on Judaism, the Bible, archeology, Jewish and Israeli poetry, and philosophy. As I reached the last shelf, I paused. The books did not seem to belong there. They were novels: The Razor's Edge by W. Somerset Maugham, Not So Wild a Dream by Eric Severaid, The Web and the Rock by Thomas Wolfe, and The Alexandria Quartet by Lawrence Durrell.

Eden walked by at that moment and noticed my puzzled expression. "Don't think Asher is limited to only Jewish sources in his quest for knowledge and truth," she said. "His love of secular literature was one of the early points of contention between him and my father." She came over and gently touched the spine of Justine, a volume in Durrell's series. "Personally, Maugham is one of my favorites." She said it with a certain fondness, almost a wistfulness. And with that, she limped from the room. A few minutes later I heard the stairs creak as the rabbi came down to continue our conversation.

# 16

## Berlin

We sat down at the living room table. The rabbi commented on how he loved his naps because they contained vivid dreams detached from time. I could not resist telling him about my David dreams, which I had been meaning to ask him about. He said that the statue of David represented Judaism, which was reaching out to me even at a young age. As in the dream, my parents had brought me so far, but then I was on my own. He said that he thought he understood the scene in the Temple with the goat, but he wanted to wait before he tried to explain it to me.

"Rabbi," I asked. "Did Einstein ever come to you and tell you his dreams?"

"Once. And I will never forget it. He couldn't sleep one night because of a dream and he came to talk to me about it. It was not long after his beloved sister Maja had died. In the dream he saw her dress on a chair. He tried to fold it but was unable to do so. Suddenly, the dress disappeared and one of his friends appeared in its place."

"What did you tell him the dream meant?"

"I probably should not have told you his dream. So let me leave it at that. And I will not let you know where his ashes are scattered either."

"You know where they are?" I said in disbelief. "I thought no one knows!"

"A few of us do, including Eden."

Eden brought us a blue box of Horowitz-Margareten matzoh, some gefilte fish, and a bottle of Seltzer. "This box of Matzoh has an interesting connection to Kafka," the rabbi began. "Before the Horowitz and Margareten families came to America during the last century, the Horowitz family had resided for centuries in Prague. Five hundred years ago they were one of the leading families of the Prague community and built the famous Pinchas Synagogue in 1535 that Kafka's family belonged to." The rabbi took a piece of fish and said, "In Prague, German anti-Semitism aroused Albert's Jewishness, but it was after he arrived in Berlin in 1914 that his Jewish identity became anchored in his psyche. 'When I came to Germany,' he once told me, 'I discovered for the first time that I was a Jew, and I owe this discovery more to the Gentiles than to the Jews.' This discovery was tied to the foul tide of anti-Semitism that was slowly bringing its stench into German society. It was in Germany that Albert began to be, as he said to me once, 'fully aware of our precarious situation.'"

"Was there a moment, or an incident, that made it clear to Einstein that it was time to go?" I asked.

"Yes. In the fall of 1919, a joint meeting of the Royal Society and Royal Astronomical Society in London announced that Einstein's General Theory of Relativity, which showed that light is bent by gravity, had been proven true by Sir Arthur Eddington's observations of the solar eclipse that year. With that, Einstein became famous worldwide, like rock stars today. He said, 'If my theory of relativity is proven successful, Germany will claim me as a German and France will declare that I am a citizen of the world. Should my theory prove untrue, France will say that I am a German and Germany will declare that I am a Jew.'

"It sounds as though he knew, even then, what he was up against."

"Not quite. But by the time his theory of relativity was proven true, the reaction in Germany would be different from what Albert had originally expected. In the spring of 1920, the Arbeitsgemeinschaft Deutscher Naturforscher, the Study Group of German Natural Philosophers, was organized. Its purpose was to attack Albert's scientific findings because he was Jewish. The following year Albert was awarded the Nobel Prize for Physics for his earlier work on the photoelectric effect. This was important in the understanding of light acting as both a wave and a particle, and was very important in the understanding of Quantum physics. His receiving this award actually precipitated further attacks on him by another German Nobel Prize winner, Philip Lenard. By the following year, Albert told his friend the Austrian physicist Phillip Frank that he did not expect to live in Germany longer than ten years. Albert was off by a year. As you may know, he left in 1933, just before Hitler became chancellor. He would never return to Germany and even a decade after the war criticized German Jews who returned to Germany."

"Why did he feel that way?" I asked the rabbi. "It seems a bit out of character."

"I can only speculate, but I think there were two reasons. The first was that he felt what Germany did was the most vulgar and perverted kind of nationalism. Second, I think he felt betrayed by the culture that had produced Bach, Beethoven, and Goethe. His feeling was so strong about this that he was even displeased when Martin Buber agreed to return to Germany to accept a prize."

"He must have been relieved to be in the United States," I said.

"No doubt," said the rabbi, as he spritzed some seltzer into his glass. "But while America welcomed Albert, he did not completely escape anti-Semitism here, although it was less virulent than in Germany. Princeton, then, was a bastion of Wasp privilege. Albert once said to me, 'I feel that I am not kept advised as to what is going on. There is anti-Semitism at Princeton.' Add to this his eccentric manner of dress, his unconventional views on religion, and his radical political views and one could easily see why there was a certain lack of warmth on the part of the Princeton established community. If you listened close enough, back then, you could hear whispers of this coming from certain circles in the town."

"I'm sure that part of Princeton existed," I said, "although I have never personally experienced it."

"Anti-Semitism can be subtle," said the rabbi, "but still very real. But the anti-Semitism here, except in rare instances, is nothing like what it was in Germany in the 1930s. Albert's reaction to the anti-Semitism he faced in Germany was to embrace the Zionist movement." The rabbi leaned forward in his chair. "Mind you, this embrace was qualified. Albert was averse to all nationalistic movements, and Jewish nationalism was no exception. He foresaw the clash between Zionism and the local Arab population. Nevertheless, he felt Zionism was a way of instilling Jewish dignity in the face of growing German anti-Semitism. And he was drawn to the spiritual and cultural aspects of the Zionist philosopher and thinker Achad Ha'am. He saw in Zionism the potential for a Jewish renaissance. Recalling his visit to Palestine in 1923, he told me that he considered it one of the greatest experiences of his life. He was quoted in the Palestine Weekly during that visit."

The rabbi went to his study and returned with a large folder. He searched through it. "Oh, here is something else he had to say about Zionism: 'The goal that the leaders of Zionism have in mind

105

is not a political but a social and cultural one. The Palestine community should aim to approach the social ideal of our ancestors as it is set down in the Bible and, at the same time, become a place of modern spiritual life. A spiritual center for the Jews of the entire world ...'" The rabbi rummaged in the folder again. "Ah, here it is," he said as he pulled out a faded newspaper clipping: 'Today I have been made happy by the sight of the Jewish people learning to recognize themselves and to make themselves recognized as a force in the world. This is a great age, the age of liberation of the Jewish soul; and it has been accomplished through the Zionist movement, so that no one in the world will be able to destroy it.'"

"Rabbi, what do you think he meant by the 'Jewish soul?'" I asked.

"I think, for Jews, the Jewish soul is our values, history, and collective memory, working inside us in the deepest way. It is timeless. Better, it explodes time—as Einstein did. Different peoples and cultures have their own version of it. But whoever we are, wherever we are from, whatever tradition we claim or that claims us, it is part of fully awakening as human beings to feel our souls calling us back to the source. It is a longing in all of us, like the force of gravity, like magnetic attraction—both areas in physics that obsessed Einstein. Oh, Joseph, sometimes I think he was expressing a supremely elegant theology with his brilliant formulas!

"I think it was also part of his Jewish soul that he advocated cooperation with the Arab population. This is part of our great tradition of mishpat ve tzedek, justice and righteousness. Albert told me once, 'If we do not succeed in finding the path of honest cooperation and coming to terms with the Arabs, we will not have learned anything from our two-thousand-year-old ordeal and will deserve the fate which will beset us.' He supported the idea of a bi-national solution. A group called Brit Shalom led by Rabbi Judah Magnus, who in 1925 became the first chancellor of Hebrew University, advocated this idea in Israel. In 1920, before he made aliyah to Israel, Magnus had helped found the American Civil Liberties Union, the ACLU, along with Helen Keller and Norman Thomas. Another leader in Brit Shalom was Hugo Bergmann, whom Einstein knew in Prague through Berta Fanta's salon. When the idea of a bi-national state went up in smoke with the 1948 War of Independence, Albert came to the conclusion that partition was the only solution. Nevertheless, always suspicious of nationalism, he warned that how Israel treated its Arab minority would be one of its moral tests."

"I wonder what he would think of the situation today." I said as I took a piece of matzoh.

"Einstein was an avid follower of current events. He listened to Howard K. Smith every Sunday night on the radio and the United Nations broadcast every evening at a quarter to six. In November 1953, UN Resolution 101 condemned Israel for its raid led by General Ariel Sharon on the Jordanian village of Kibya. I remember Albert saying a few days later that he agreed with the UN's reprimand of Israel for the raid. I did not disagree with the resolution, I told him, but reminded him that the resolution also called upon Jordan to keep up its end of the bargain of stopping infiltrators from coming into Israel and killing people. He then commented on how part of the Arab opposition to Israel was to deflect attention from the internal dissatisfactions within their own countries."

"That's true," I said.

"Still, it is no excuse. In the 1920s, Albert was disturbed by the exclusion of many Jewish students from universities throughout much of Europe. I am not sure if he was aware of the quota system here in America, which limited the number of Jewish students that could attend universities. And even after those quotas were eliminated, more subtle forms of exclusionary practices continued.

"Because of what Albert knew was happening in Europe, the idea of the founding of Hebrew University in Jerusalem became of great interest to him. In 1921, he accompanied Zionist leader and fellow scientist Chaim Weizman on a tour of the United States to raise funds for the Zionist movement and, in particular, for the Hebrew University. For the next three and a half decades he would be Zionism's most famous advocate, working many hours for the advancement of the Zionist cause. When the World's Fair was held in New York in 1939, it was Einstein who opened the Palestine pavilion. In 1952, following the death of Weizman, he was asked to become the second President of Israel."

"And what happened?" I asked, excited.

"He refused."

"Why?" I asked. What a grand notion! Einstein, president of Israel.

"I know," chuckled the rabbi. "The idea had charm for me as well. But it's probably just as well. Einstein said he was moved by the offer, but declined it because, as he put it, 'I know a little about nature and hardly anything about men.'"

"Rabbi," I asked, "I have always had this question about Zionism and the birth of Israel: Why should a religion get its own nation?"

"Because you live after Napoleon," he said. Seeing the puzzled look on my face, he continued, "Wait here a moment and I will get you the beginning of the answer." He rose again from his chair, went into his study and returned with a siddur, a prayer book. "Joseph, what is this?"

"A siddur," I answered.

"Correct, and what is its function?"

"To outline the prayer services for us."

"Good. What else?"

"To bring us closer to God."

"Yes, and what else?"

I knew that he was leading me somewhere but I could not figure out where.

"Joseph, what you are holding in your hands was one of the repositories of a seed of an idea, a memory, a hope that was carried for almost two thousand years. It was held in our collective soul for generations, waiting to for the right conditions to germinate.

"Eden," he called out, "why don't you take over here." Turning to me he said, "Eden earned her Ph.D. in Zionist Studies. Her thesis was "Three Generations of Women in Kibbutz Living: Case Studies." We have a granddaughter who helped found Kibbutz Ketura in the southern Arava three and a half years ago."

Eden sat down next to the rabbi and began. "After the Romans put down the Bar Kochba Revolt in 135 C.E. and ended any hope of Jewish Independence, they changed Israel's name to Palestine as part of their policy of eliminating all Jewish connections to the land. By the way, the name 'Palestine' was taken from the Philistines, a sea-faring people from the Aegean Sea who reached the coast of Israel in the Late Bronze Age and settled in the area around the Gaza Strip. The rabbis knew of this plan to eliminate our connection to the land, therefore the numerous reminders of our connection to the land in the liturgy was further codified and strengthened as time went on. This included the many daily reminders in the siddur about Israel, her land, and restoration of Jewish independence.

"In addition, some holidays further remind us of our connection to the land. Think about it: Celebrating Tu B'Shvat, the Jewish holiday of trees, makes no sense in January in the middle of the winter in New England, or Warsaw, or Berlin. We know of no other people who were exiled from their land for more than a hundred and fifty years and maintained both their identity and connection to that land. And we did it for almost two thousand years. We were able to do it because we consciously kept that connection strong. It's an amazing story and beautiful accomplishment when you think about it."

"Yes, but I still don't understand why a religion should get its own country?"

"Asher, could you please put some tea on," Eden said before answering my question. The rabbi got up and went into the kitchen to boil some water. "This brings us to Napoleon, but before we get to him you need to understand a few other things. For almost eighteen hundred years this seed lay dormant in our prayers, our holidays, and our siddur. Then, about two hundred years ago, two important revolutions began to create the right conditions for that seed to germinate. The American Revolution of 1776, with its idea of freedom, and some ten years later the French Revolution of 1789, with its call for Liberté, Egalité, et Fraternité; and The Declaration of the Rights of Man and of the Citizen brought about profound changes, particularly in Europe.

"Out of these events, along with the Enlightenment of the second half of the eighteenth century and the Romantic ideas of the early nineteenth century, the idea of the modern nation-state began to take shape. This idea would influence not only Zionism but also Pan-Arabism and Pan-Turkism as well. During the nineteenth century the Italian federations joined together to became Italy, the German federations formed Germany, and Greece, Serbia, and Montenegro became independent. These nations were made up of citizens who were also given new rights. A question that could not be avoided was, 'What about the Jews?' And now we get to your question."

The rabbi returned carrying a small tray with a pot of tea,

cups and saucers, a small matching container for milk and another one for sugar. He poured tea for each of us, and we each took what of the milk and sugar that we wanted. He sat down and joined us.

Eden continued. "In 1806 Napoleon called a meeting of the Assembly of Jewish Notables and put the question to them, 'Are Jews a member of a religion or a nation?' This was followed the next year by a meeting of a 'Great Sanhedrin' that included rabbis and lay leaders. Behind the question was the understanding that each nation was established for the citizens of that particular nation. The notion of the melting pot and mass migrations that we saw at the end of the last century and throughout this century had not yet occurred. These Jewish leaders understood the question and the ramifications of their answer. If they said a nation, then there would be complications. If they said a religion, then Jews could be welcomed as citizens. And that is exactly what they said. It was one of many compromises to Jewish identity that Jews would make during the next hundred years in order to be accepted by the larger society. And to a large degree it worked, as Jews were granted more and more rights, gathering extra momentum after the revolutions of 1848.

"This is why most people today think of Jews as members of a religion, but the truth is that that is a truncated understanding of who we are. In 1942, Martin Buber wrote a beautiful essay called "Hebrew Humanism" in which he addresses that particular self-identification."

"Dear I'll get the copy from my study," the rabbi said to Eden as he got up from the table. He returned with Arthur Hertzberg's The Zionist Idea and handed it to Eden, who opened to Buber's essay. She began to read:

"'Israel is not a nation like other nations, no matter how much its representatives have wished it during certain eras.'" She paused, looked up from the book, and said to me, "This was addressed directly to the decision of the 'Great Sanhedrin' of Napoleon." She then continued, "'Israel is a people like no other, for it is the only people in the world which, from its earliest beginnings, has been both a nation and a religious community. In the historical hour in which its tribes grew together to form a people, it became the carrier of a revelation ... Israel was and is a people and a religious community in one, and it is this unity which has enabled it to survive in an exile no other nation had to suffer, an exile which lasted much longer than the period of its independence. He who severs this bond severs the life of Israel.'

"So Joseph," added Eden, "being a member of the Jewish people means being a member of both a religion and a nation at the same time."

"I like that notion," I said. "But what about that seed you mentioned? When did Zionism begin to bloom?"

"Unlike most seeds that germinate when conditions are nice," she said, "and the weather turns warmer and the rains bring their life-affirming water, the conditions for Zionism's growth were a reaction to the dark clouds of intolerance that began to blow once again across Europe. While Jews were being welcomed in more and more countries, particularly in Western Europe, it was often done with the mixed message of, 'But please don't be too Jewish.' By the end of the nineteenth century a new anti-Semitism was starting to ferment across Europe. In Russia a series of pogroms in the 1880s lead to the formation of B.I.L.U., whose name was derived from the Hebrew of a line from Isaiah, 'O House of Jacob, come let us go,' and Chovevi Zion, which advocated for the return of Jews to the Land of Israel. Finally, in 1894 Alfred Dreyfus, a Jewish officer in the French army, was falsely charged and convicted of spying. The charges were trumped up solely because he was Jewish, and his case became a cause célèbre. Emile Zola wrote his famous article

"J'Accuse" in which he accused the French authorities of anti-Semitism. By the way, Zola had also come to his friend Manet's defense thirty years earlier when Manet's style of painting had been attacked. Dreyfus was retried in 1899 and found guilty again but was pardoned by the French president. In 1906 he was completely exonerated.

"A secular Jewish Austrian reporter for the Neue Freie Presse by the name of Theodore Herzl was sent to Paris to cover the trial. The trial had a profound effect on him. He concluded that if all these other peoples had their own nations, it was time for the Jews to also have their own homeland in which they would be free from persecution and once again be able to build a Jewish culture. In 1895 Herzl wrote Der Judenstadt, The Jewish State. He wrote it while living at the Hotel de Castille on Rue Cambon, in the heart of the fashionable First Arrondissement a few blocks from the Louvre, the Opera House, and the Place Vendome, It was published the following year, and in 1897 the First Zionist Congress was held in Basel, and the modern Zionist movement was born. And so this incredible idea that the Jewish people had a right to return to their homeland as a free people, which lay dormant while being nurtured by the Jewish people for almost two thousand years, was germinated by the combination of the revolutions of 1776 and 1786, modern nationalism, and modern anti-Semitism."

"There is one interesting footnote to all of this," the rabbi chimed in, a mischievous look in his eye. "Both Herzl and Freud lived on the same street in Vienna. Can you imagine if Herzl had told Freud about his Zionist dream?" He then said, laughing, "Freud would have told him that he was suffering from an enlarged ego and that he should drop the idea!

"Because of the anti-Semitism that was rife in Europe," the rabbi continued, "Albert understood the need for a Jewish homeland—and, as I mentioned, he actively campaigned for it. His visit to America in 1921 on behalf of the Zionist movement was a sensation. It had the same electricity the Beatles generated when they first came to the States in 1964. Einstein was a star, constantly followed by the media. He even met with President Harding. His visit instilled a deep sense of pride in the Jewish American community. Recalling that first visit to America, he once told me how he was struck by the Jews from Eastern Europe who had immigrated to the United States. Disparaged by the Jews of Western Europe, particularly those of Germany, they still retained, in his eyes, a healthy connection to Judaism. He also found in them an extraordinary readiness 'for self-sacrifice and practical creativity.' Albert said they had a passion for learning and self-improvement. That desire for knowledge, though often religiously based, struck a chord with his curious, scientific mind."

"My own family was part of the exodus," I said.

"Eastern European and Russian Jewry have played an important role in shaping the American Jewish character," the rabbi said. "In Germany, Albert painfully witnessed the Jewish people externally attacked," he continued. "I think that he was quite right in his observation that 'Jewish solidarity is another invention of their enemies.' All of this caused him to reflect deeply on what being Jewish meant to him personally. As time went on, it became clearer and clearer that most of his views and passions went hand in hand with Judaism. For Albert, being in Berlin completed the process that began in Prague, where he could not ignore his Jewish heritage, even if he acknowledged it reluctantly. In Berlin, he finally embraced it."

The rabbi leaned back in his chair. "I'm sorry," he said. "I have once again gone on for a long time. Do you have any questions, or shall we stop?"

"No, please continue," I said. "In what ways did Einstein's

views and those of Judaism go hand in hand?"

"Often Albert told me that 'pursuit of knowledge for its own sake, an almost fanatical love of justice, and the desire for personal independence—these are the features of Jewish tradition which make me thank the stars that I belong to it.' Albert was a socialist in his political outlook, a believer in world government, as well as an active pacifist from World War I onwards. The exception to this was World War II, which he believed, although it saddened him, was a justified and unavoidable war. For forty years, he campaigned for and was a member of numerous pacifist organizations, working publicly with fellow pacifists like Sigmund Freud and Bertrand Russell. In 1955, shortly before his death, he co-signed the Russell-Einstein manifesto, which called for nuclear disarmament. Albert had come to Russell's support decades earlier when Russell's Marriage and Morals was considered too shocking and Russell was fired from his position at the City College of New York. Such censorship smacked too much of what Albert had experienced in Germany. He wrote to Russell, who he also considered to be the best living writer of the time, in verse: 'In this world the so fine and honest/the parson alarms the populace/The genius is executed.' Others were uncomfortable not only with Russell but also with Albert. I once overheard someone when I was out for a stroll say, 'How dare the nudist Russell and the refugee Einstein interfere in the family life of the United States!'

"His famous letter to President Roosevelt in August 1939, warning him of the possibility of the Nazis' production of a nuclear bomb, was motivated by his belief that in certain situations, 'Organized power can be opposed only by organized power.' Of course it was his discovery of $E = mc2$ that gave the world the understanding that mass and energy can be interchangeable, leading to the development of nuclear power. However, once Germany was defeated he saw no reason for the bomb to be used.

"Albert also threw himself into civil rights before it was a popular cause in the United States. When the black singer Marian Anderson was denied a room in one of Princeton's hotels, Albert invited her to stay at his home."

"But Rabbi, I also know from my political science class that many Americans read the Bible in such a way as to justify slavery, saying that blacks were the cursed descendents of Noah's son Ham. So how can we use the Bible if it can be used to justify such actions?"

"And Martin Luther King," the rabbi said, "used the Bible as both the justification and inspiration to challenge a racist society. So if the Bible can be used to justify both sides of the same issue, where does that leave us? Joseph, living a moral life is the key to salvation. Yes the Bible is one of our most important sources in that regard. My friend Rabbi Ira Eisenstein would say that it requires a combination of experience, intuition, and reason."

"But those can all be objective?"

"Correct, I would say that the Golden Rule of Hillel, 'What is hateful to you, do not do to your neighbor' is the litmus test for all interpretations of the Torah. If it fails that test, it fails.

"Let's return to Albert's political activity," the rabbi said as he adjusted the pillow behind his back. "Albert was also a champion of individual rights and publicly supported individuals who refused to testify in front of the House Un-American Activities Committee. He also championed Oppenheimer, 'the father of the bomb,' who at the time was the Director of the Institute for Advanced Study and was accused of treason. Representative John Rankin, a member of the House Un-American Activities Committee, said, 'It's about time the American people got wise to Einstein ... He ought to be prosecuted.' In numerous instances, he worked on the cases of Jewish refugees from Europe who were looking for ways to escape Hitler's lethal grip."

I asked, "How did Einstein deal with all the attention?"

"He once said to me, 'Why is it that nobody understands me and everybody likes me?' In many ways he would have preferred the solitary life in a lighthouse isolated from all the distractions that fame brought him. Despite that desire he was the kindest, most generous and understanding man in the world. Over the years, he wrote literally thousands of letters supporting people in need, and gave advice to hundreds more, in person and on the phone, even when he doubted their stories."

"How was he able to involve himself in so many large causes and still have time for so many individual people with their everyday problems?" I asked.

The rabbi chuckled. "It was one of his gifts," he said as he passed Eden some pungent freshly ground horseradish. "Albert was a radical with a heart. He wrote once to his lifelong friend, Elisabeth the Queen Mother of Belgium, 'I have become a kind of enfant terrible in my new homeland, due to my inability to keep silent and to swallow everything that happens there.' There were people who wrote to him that he would end up in hell because of his position on religion; there were others who prayed for his soul. He once told me that he was 'an old revolutionary, a politically fire-spewing Mount Vesuvius.' He even was known to sign a letter once, 'A Subversive.'

"His sister, Maja, once showed me a letter in which Albert had written, 'After all, the foundation of all human values is morality. To have recognized this clearly in primitive times is the unique greatness of our Moses.' After Albert's death, Rabbi Yehuda Cohen sent me a copy of a memorial service that was held in honor of Albert in Los Angeles. Let me see where it is ..." he said, searching through the folder. "Here. At that service one of the speakers said, 'If the prophets of the Bible cried out for social justice, he was their spiritual descendant. When they exalted the concept of human dignity and value, their words, across the bridge of centuries, echoed in his heart and came to his tongue. If he, as a scientist, sought absolutes and fundamentals, he detected them too in the basic structure of Jewish religious thought ... The bond that has united the Jews for thousands of years and unites them today, Einstein said, is, above all, the democratic ideal of social justice coupled with the ideal of mutual aid and tolerance among all people. Even the most religious scriptures of Jews are steeped in this social ideal, which so powerfully affected Christianity and Mohammedanism, and has had a benign influence upon the social structure of a great part of humanity.'"

The rabbi put the speech back in the folder and pulled out a typed piece of paper. "Albert shared this essay with me shortly after he turned down Ben-Gurion's offer to become the second President of Israel following the death of Chaim Weizman." The rabbi began to read from the one-page typed essay, 'To me, the Torah and the Talmud are merely the most important evidence of the manner in which the Jewish conception of life held sway in earlier times ... the essence of that conception seems to me to lie in an affirmative attitude to the life of all creation. The life of the individual only has meaning in so far as it aids in making the life of every living thing nobler and more beautiful. Life is sacred, that is to say, it is the supreme value, to which other values are subordinate. The hallowing of the supra-individual life brings in its train a reverence for everything spiritual—a particularly characteristic feature of the Jewish tradition. Judaism is not a creed: the Jewish God is simply a negation of superstition, an imaginary result of its elimination. It is also an attempt to base the moral law on fear, a regrettable and discreditable attempt. Yet it seems to me that the strong moral tradition of the Jewish nation has to a large extent shaken itself from this fear. It is clear also that 'serving God' was equated with 'serving the living.'" The rabbi put the essay back in the folder.

Before he could continue, I said, "Einstein said Judaism, in large part, has eliminated fear from its spirituality. But I always thought the message of the Bible was all about fear. God was fire and brimstone and you'd better fear him or else!"

"Ah, yes," said the rabbi. "That notion is well established: Judaism is a religion of fear and Christianity is the religion of love. Like Jesus saying to turn the other check."

"Exactly," I said.

"And where do you think he got that idea from?"

"I thought it was his quote."

"Yes, it's his quote but he was actually paraphrasing something Isaiah said some seven hundred years earlier."

"I didn't know that."

"Most people don't, and that is part of the problem; however, it is also easy to see why there is the fear/love view of the two traditions. In Tanach, the Jewish Bible, the obligation to fear God appears more times than to love God. But fortunately Judaism did not end with the Bible; it continued and has continued to evolve. By the time of the Talmud, the rabbis had staked out a clear preference for love over fear. Rabbi Simeon ben Eleazar taught: 'Greater is the one who acts from love than the one who acts from fear.' That is not to say that the notion of fear of God was done away with in Judaism, but it was understood through different perspectives."

"Did you and Einstein discuss this?" I asked.

"Of course! I tried to get Albert to understand that fear has a function that we should not so easily dismiss. One morning, Albert and I were sitting in front of Nassau Hall on the steps between the two tiger statues. I said to him that there is a certain hubris in thinking there should be no fear when it comes to God. To truly encounter the Life Force, the Creator, the mysterium tremendum of Being and of the entire Universe is no light matter. We are not talking about a 50 watt soft white light bulb here."

I laughed at that image.

The rabbi continued, "There is another issue here as well. The Hebrew word that we are talking about is yirah. It can mean 'fear.' But it can also mean 'awe.' So for example Psalm 111 means 'the awe of God is the beginning of wisdom,' and not, as is it is too often translated, 'the fear of God is the beginning of wisdom.' As Heschel said, 'Awe is a way of being in rapport with the mystery of all reality' and 'Awe, unlike fear, does not make us shrink from the awe-inspiring object, but, on the contrary, draws us near to it. This is why awe is compatible with both love and joy. In a sense, awe is the antithesis of fear.'"

"Hmm," I said, "Awe and fear, the antithesis of each other, yet both the same word in Hebrew ... interesting." I felt as though I had found an important key to one of the many doors I needed to walk through.

The rabbi nodded, then picked up where he had left off before our little digression over the issue of fear: "Albert loved to tell people about an incident which exemplified the sanctity of life to the Jewish people. He once remarked to a friend, 'When a Jew says that he's going hunting to amuse himself, he lies.' For Albert, the Jewish sense of the sanctity of life could not have been more simply expressed.

"On another occasion, Albert told me, 'For me, the essence of religion is to be capable of putting oneself in the skin of another human being, to rejoice in his joy and to suffer in his suffering ... Only a life lived for others is a life worthwhile.' Or as we read in the Mishna: 'Do not judge your fellow human being till you stand in their situation.'

"Joseph, let me give you another teaching. The Hebrew word for mercy is rachamim, which at its core is rechem, which is womb. When a woman is pregnant she must also think of the needs of an other. When Moses wants to see God's face, Moses is told that he can't. Rather, God tells him to move to a cleft in the rock on top of Mount Sinai and God will pass by, showing God's back. At that moment, God also talks about His trait of mercy. What is mercy? The ability to see the world from the perspective of someone else, as though you are peering over their shoulder and seeing the world as they do."

"I will remember that," I replied. "I can see this as a universal Jewish moral attitude. But did Einstein also have a view of Judaism that was more Judeo-centered?"

"I am so glad that I saved all these writings of Albert's," the rabbi said as he searched through the file. "I knew at some point people would begin to take an interest in Albert's Judaism and its relationship to his development and thinking as a scientist. Ah, here is what I was looking for, which may answer your question, although I don't remember when he wrote this to me. 'A characteristic trait of Jewish tradition is the high regard in which it holds every form of intellectual aspiration and spiritual effort. I am convinced that this great respect for intellectual striving is solely responsible for the contribution that Jews have made toward the progress of knowledge, in the broadest sense of the term.'

"About the Nazis he said in 1932, 'History has imposed upon us a severe struggle. But as long as we remain devoted servants of truth, justice, and freedom, we shall not only continue to exist as the oldest living peoples, but we shall also, as hitherto, create through productive effort values which shall contribute to the ennobling of mankind.' I once asked Albert what he would do if he arrived in a strange town and the police registration form was put in front of him and he was required to indicate his religious affiliation. Einstein replied, 'In this case I should put Jewish, for here is the question of a brotherhood of fate.'"

The rabbi had talked for a long time, and I was worried that I had exhausted him. I asked whether I could return the following morning to continue our conversation—but it was not to be.

When I arrived at the door, Eden was leaving the house with the weight of concern on her face. "Oh, Joseph, I am sorry that I didn't call," she said, struggling against tears. "Last night, Asher had a heart attack. His brother is a cardiologist, and we have been monitoring this possibility for a long time. As soon as it started, we were able to get him to the hospital. He should be all right." And then she started to cry as the floodgate of worry overcame her. I hugged her and began to cry, too.

Wiping the tears from her face with a handkerchief, she said, "Joseph, as much as Asher would love to see you, he will need to rest without visitors. I will send him your love." She locked the door to the house and then got into a waiting taxi. I stood alone on the porch and watched the taxi drive away.

That night in the dream, David turned away from me. I tried to follow him, but I felt that odd paralysis we sometimes have in dreams. I couldn't move. I tried to reach out to him, but he receded into darkness.

# 17

## September 11th

It was almost twenty-five years later and I found myself in New York City. I had received a sabbatical from my congregation in rural Vermont along with a grant from the Bruce and Nora Davis Family Foundation in Chicago. The grant was to study the feasibility of taking the Biblical concept of the sabbatical year and applying it beyond the usual recipients of clergy and professors to the larger American workforce. I was going to do research for four months and then go to Israel in January with my family where we would get an apartment in Jerusalem and I would write up my research.

I was in New York to visit the offices of a number of Blue Chip companies as well as other business firms. My first day had been worthwhile as I explored with a former Fortune 500 executive, over a delicious Italian lunch at Café Grazie on the Upper East Side, the concept of staggering the workforce by seven so that one seventh of the workforce would have a sabbatical each year. As we finished lunch with a lemon tart and an espresso he suggested a few people who I should meet during the upcoming months.

The next day I had a number of meetings scheduled down in Wall Street. Since the restaurant was a few blocks from the Metropolitan Museum of Art I decided to take the afternoon and visit her galleries. I particularly like looking at paintings of Biblical scenes. Each painting is an interpretation of the text. I use post cards that I have collected from different museums to teach Biblical commentary. My favorite exercise is to get more than one painting of the same scene and examine the different ways it has been painted, the different ways it has been interpreted, and discuss what we learn from those different explanations of the text.

One of the best parts of the sabbatical was that I was going to get to spend a lot of time in New York, which would also include taking advantage of its many Jewish institutions and activities. There is no city in the world like New York. Stepping onto the island of Manhattan, one immediately experiences a pulsating energy that is located from the heights of its buildings that scrape the sky down to its subways that tunnel their way through its rock and soil. New York pounces upon all of one's senses. It is this stimulation that is the fabric from which so much culture and creativity emerge.

New York is loud. There is the constant backdrop of car horns, police and ambulance sirens, and a subway system that does not know the word quiet. Roasted chestnuts and peanuts sold by street vendors perfume the air along with a blend of smells from around the world emanating from its hundreds of restaurants. There are certain tastes that are only found in New York, like New York City bagels. There is one theory that their unique taste comes from using New York City water. And then there is vision. New York stands tall with its skyscrapers elevating all who work in them or gaze at their reach upwards. From its brownstones to its apartment buildings to its office buildings, diverse architectural styles are laid out for the eyes to feast upon.

And then there are the people. They keep the city open twenty-four hours a day. They are the notes to an unending jazz riff, colored by yellow taxis and the red, yellow, and green of traffic lights that move up and down its avenues and across its streets, setting its tempo all day and all night. New York is picking up a copy of the next day's the New York Times before that day has even begun. New York is about confidence, sometimes brash, like the Yankees baseball team. New York is homage to the possibility of what human effort and creativity can be all about.

As I walked through the museum I noticed that it was getting darker and darker outside. I walked out the museum and down 5th Avenue for a few blocks to catch the 79 cross-town bus at 79th Street. It was raining, coming down harder and harder with each footstep. I boarded the bus as the first explosion of thunder echoed across the island. The rain, then a downpour, quickly changed into a deluge, creating the feel of a tropical rainforest. I said the bracha for thunder and lightning as the bus made its way across Central Park. There was something primordial about this storm, and I reveled in its natural power in this city of so much steel and concrete.

Once at Broadway I transferred to the 104 bus and took it down towards Lincoln Center near where I was staying with my cousin and her husband. I arrived soaked and changed my clothes. We took in the end of the storm from their forty-fifth-floor apartment over a takeout Chinese dinner they had called in. Once the storm had passed, the air was clean and the city appeared sharp and crisp for the evening.

I woke up the next morning to a perfect, cloudless, blue sky made possible by the previous day's storm. I was excited about my meetings that I had scheduled for the day. Getting on the 1-9 Subway at around 8:30 a.m. I headed downtown towards Wall Street. About fifteen minutes later we were told there was a delay. I thought to myself, I can't believe that I'm going to be late for my meeting. I could see by the expressions other people had on their faces that they were thinking the same thing. After a short while we were told that there was an "emergency situation at the World Trade

Center" and that the train was going to go straight to the end of the line at South Ferry. We could then hear sirens above, heading downtown. Shortly afterwards we were told that the train was going to be rerouted to Brooklyn. I thought, I'm never going to make my meeting now for sure.

But the train stopped at the Chambers Street station at West Broadway a few blocks north of the World Trade Center and so I got off the train thinking I would then walk to my appointments. As I climbed the stairs I noticed again how brilliant blue the sky was that morning, but also how everyone was looking up and behind me. When I got to the top of the steps I turned around and then froze. I stood there for minutes unable to move. I will never forget the sight of those two wounded buildings, slowly dying as they continued to smoke and burn. There was no memory file, no other experience, no other previous sensory sight to latch on to. It was like learning a completely foreign language for the first time. There was nothing to relate it to.

There was that deep groan from Tower Two as it tilted slightly and then fell in on itself. It was grotesque to see its outer skeleton stand for a few seconds and then follow the rest down in a roar and rumble of thunder and a freight train. To see something that large, that strong, that permanent come tumbling down shook the core of my being. I felt at that moment that there was nothing left in this world that I, that we, could count on with that assurance that it would be there when we needed it. There was no time for faith at that moment. I ran with the crowds as the volcanic-like cloud of the pulverized building came rolling up the city canyons towards us. I then made my way uptown with the thousands of other refugees who filled the great Avenues of New York in an exodus like no other.

I returned to New York fifteen days later for Yom Kippur.

126

New York was still raw from the attack. Since I was on sabbatical and had no High Holiday duties that year I had volunteered to work with the Red Cross at their Family Assistance Center, which had been set up at Pier 94 on the Hudson River at 54th Street.

The Pier had been transformed into a city within a city. There the magnitude of the events of September 11th become even clearer. Not only were the families of those who died there, but the thousands who lost their jobs or their homes. A labyrinth of services were available under its huge roof: insurance companies; lawyers to help process death certificates and other legal documents; police to collect DNA samples. The Red Cross was there, FEMA was there, the FBI was there, the INS was there, to mention a few. There was also free food, telephones, Internet, and a colorful childcare area for those who came to seek aid.

I was reminded of something that took on a new meaning while I prayed the evening Kol Nidre Yom Kippur service to myself that night in an area of the Pier set up for prayer and meditation. The Thirteen Attributes of God, which forms a central part of the High Holiday liturgy (Exodus 34:6-7), reminds us that God's mercy lasts for two thousand generations, while the wrong deeds of humans may last three or four generations; a ratio of 2,000 to 4 of good outlasting, outshining evil and bad. The activity under that large roof of Pier 94 was a reminder of that 500:1 ratio and reality.

I and the other clergy spoke with family members, people who had lost their homes or livelihood. We also spoke with the firefighters, police officers, lawyers, insurance agents, and the host of others who had come, sometimes from across the country, to be there to help. Conversations were sometimes very short and sometimes very long, but always filled with ever-present magnitude and thread of the reality that has brought us together.

Sometime in the early afternoon I was requested by an

insurance agent to speak with a man who had lost his son in one of the Towers. I sat down in a temporary cubical alone with the man and began to listen to him. Before long he was blaming the Jews for the attack and the death of the son. The attacks happened, he said, because the Jews had too much power in America. The Jew in me wanted to stand up and scream at him, but the rabbi in me knew that that was not the role I was there for. I slowly and patiently brought the conversation back to his grief and the loss of his son.

I left the conversation shaken and placed my hands to my lowered head, made heavy by the burden and weight of the conversation. I found my way to one of the doors of the pier and sat outside in the fresh air. A U.S. Coast Guard ship patrolled nearby. I stared at the water of the river, the afternoon sun dancing in its movement. I was numb. It was more than just the painful conversation I had been through. The conversation opened a floodgate of thoughts that I had suppressed throughout the two weeks since the attacks.

Why had I not turned around after the second tower fell to help? A local priest, who was a good friend of mine, said that when he saw what had happened while watching the television he knew immediately that only a religious-inspired person could have done such a thing. What was I doing involved in a profession that could inspire and justify madness? In all my years I never thought that I would have to pause and ask myself if it was the right choice to bring children into this world. To my horror I found myself asking that question.

I gave out a big sigh as the weight of all the questions became too heavy to bear. I closed my eyes and leaned my head on the side of the building in a vain attempt to forget it all. I soon found myself weeping as I released the growing tension within. And then I remembered that conversation that I had had with the rabbi after he had come home from the hospital after his heart attack; that conversation that in many ways had changed my life. I sat there going over and over it, my memory of his words feeding my hungry soul.

I stood up with a renewed determination. Near the end of the afternoon I had a conversation with a woman who was six months pregnant. She and her husband had an apartment near the World Trade Center that they had not been back to since the 11th. They had been told that it had been damaged as the towers collapsed. She was there to start the paperwork that they needed to do to get assistance. As I walked her outside to get a taxi I asked her if they had decided on a name. She said that they hadn't. A taxi pulled up and she got in. As the taxi began to drive away I tapped on her window. The taxi stopped and she rolled down the window, "If it's a girl, think about Hope for a name. We need more hope in this world." She smiled at me, and the taxi drove away.

As the day came to a close I stood with some of the clergy. A Russian Orthodox priest called out, "Tekiya Gedola" and I blew the Shofar's long whole note signifying the end of Yom Kippur. I left the building and broke the fast as I waited for one of the city shuttle buses to take others and me to Penn Station.

The eating of food after Yom Kippur, among many things, is also an affirmation of life and survival. I sat on the bus as it made its way through the lit-up streets and avenues of New York and began to think of the holiday of Sukkot that would begin five days later. Its message of the frailty of life as well as the need to build and rebuild took on deeper significance that year. I looked forward to building our Sukkah, no matter how fragile it might be.

# 18

## Zion and Cosmic Religion

The rabbi stayed in the hospital for six days. The first weekend after he was released, I came home from college to visit him. My parents were surprised, to say the least, to see me home so soon after my last visit.

I stopped by the rabbi's late that Saturday afternoon. Eden greeted me at the door with a big hug and showed me into the living room, where the rabbi was sitting in his comfortable reading chair.

He looked up from his book: "Joseph, you are doing a great mitzvah. It is called bikur cholim, visiting the sick. It must be working; I feel better just seeing you."

"It's so good to see you, rabbi," I responded. "I've been so worried!"

The rabbi studied me carefully.

"Yes," he finally said. "There is still much that I need to tell you ..." he lowered his voice, "to teach you."

I blushed with pleasure and gratitude. The rabbi looked as though he had lost some weight and some strength, but not his spirit. His brush with death seemed to bring on a greater urgency in what he wanted to convey to me. He said that for a short while his memory was not working as well as it should have. "It reminds me," he said, "of when I got a call one day from Albert: 'Perhaps you can tell me where Dr. Einstein lives.' I told him that I could not do that. In a near whisper he continued, 'Please don't tell anybody, but I am Dr. Einstein. I am on my way home and have forgotten where my house is.'"

"Really, he forgot where his house was?"

"It happened occasionally," said the rabbi.

We dove back into our conversation on Einstein's theology.

"We've discussed," the rabbi said, "'that deeply emotional conviction of the presence of a superior reasoning power revealed in the incomprehensible universe' that formed Albert's idea of God. More conventionally, it would be designated as pantheistic or, as you might know, the God of Spinoza."

"Then Einstein believed in God the creator?"

"Exactly. But he refused to admit to a personal God who would reward and punish the beings that He had created—a God who could be reached by prayer or angered by the neglect of some rite. He recognized the existence of a force superior to our lives, or, as he often put it, 'I believe in Spinoza's God who reveals himself in the orderly harmony of what exists, not in a God who concerns Himself with the fates and the actions of human beings.'"

"So if he did not believe in a personal God," I asked, "then what could be the function of prayer?" Internally, I realized that I felt uncomfortable, not with the attitude of blessing to which the rabbi had introduced me, but the thought of what I felt could only be contrived words on my part, ineffectually reaching toward the divine.

"Too often," said the rabbi, leaning closer to me, "when we are not raised with prayer, it can seem phony, almost silly—a false comfort in our state of existential aloneness. We think of prayer as asking God to change something in our life. Often the object of our prayer is something external, and here I mean something external

131

from our soul, like good health, or changing a situation in which we find ourselves. But prayer can be more sophisticated than that. It can be about giving us the internal strength to deal with what we face externally in our life. Rabbi Scrod reminds us in his teaching that when we ask God for forgiveness, three times a day, we are invoking the power of our ancient sacrificial system: 'to burn it up and let it go!' With that approach we understand that religion can be about guilt relief, and not instilling guilt. Prayer gives us moments in the day to examine what we have done, and not to get stuck in our short-comings, but rather recognize them and try to deal with them—and then move on. Religion does not exist so that we can escape from our problems. On the contrary, religion is the place for us to focus on them—confronting them within the powerful context of the concentric existential circles of Torah, God, and our history."

The rabbi was speaking with a kind of urgency that I had not heard before, and he pounded the table to emphasize his point: "Religion should not be demoted, as it too often is, to a balm to soothe over life's problems. Religion is not a palliative. It is the address, the framework where we encounter life, not where we try to circumvent it. Kaplan adds an important insight here, 'Religion is not intended to answer the ultimate questions of existence. It can only provide an effective protection against their shattering impact.' Prayer is a technique to confront the existential. Yes, religion serves to comfort as well, but on a deeper level it is about struggle, work, the effort required for spiritual growth. Being human is not only about living a good life. That is certainly a goal, but it is not the only goal. Living a good life is the external goal, but there is another goal to our lives, as I have said to you before, which is more internal: It is about living a full, meaningful life; it's about nurturing the soul, and connecting our lives to the Unifying Source of the Universe. If our bodies need air, then our souls need God. However, Judaism has never promised that God accepts all prayer. The efficacy of prayer is not the central term of inquiry in our philosophy. Rabbi Finkelstein once shared a wonderful insight on this point with me: 'When I pray, I talk to God; when I study, God speaks to me.'"

"So tell me again, why pray?" I asked.

"Rav Soloveitchik writes, 'Acceptance of prayer is a hope, a vision, a wish, a petition, but not a principle or a premise. The foundation of prayer is not the conviction of its effectiveness but the belief that through it we approach God intimately and the miraculous community embracing finite man and his Creator is born. The basic function of prayer is not its practical consequences but the metaphysical formation of a fellowship consisting of God and man.'"

The rabbi had become more and more animated as he spoke. I feared for his health, but there was no stopping him—and in truth, I didn't want to. His words rang out, inspiring me. "Religion is not just about doing good deeds," he said, reminding me of what I had heard from my grandfather many years earlier. "A mitzvah is a commandment. It is not a good deed, as it is so often translated. Part of the problem is that not everyone feels that there is a Commander commanding us. While I recognize the theological difficulty for many people, another aspect of the commandment system is also at work. Within the context of commandment there is a holy obligation. Obligation does not mean doing something when you feel like doing it, or only when it is convenient. The question is not 'When will I do it?' but 'How will I do it?' Joseph," the rabbi said, looking deep into my eyes, "you need to start asking that second question. Observance begins with sincerity and commitment.

"Joseph, I am not necessarily advocating observance of all the 613 mitzvot. Nor am I advocating a watered-down-pick-and-choose approach, as though one were choosing one's favorite ice cream flavors. I am talking about a serious process of study and examination where the individual challenges their own comfort zone and assumptions as they go through this process. We need to make Judaism relevant and meaningful again for so many of the Jews who are on the margins or who are living a diluted Jewish life."

Eden came in and placed her hand on the rabbi's shoulder and said, "Dear, please a little less excitement."

The rabbi sat back in his chair and then continued at a less spirited pace: "I will also concede that I don't understand prayer completely. For me prayer is a synapse, a junction within the Universe." He adjusted the yarmulke on his head. "I have seen too many situations in my life where people have prayed for something to be changed in their lives and it happened. I have also seen people in similar situations pray for the same thing, but with a different outcome. What we are left with is Einstein's sense of mystery. We have to live with that mystery. And that is not such a bad thing. Not knowing or understanding everything can have a healthy humbling effect on a person. A sixth-grader wrote to Albert in 1936 about prayer. He wrote back to the child." The rabbi pulled a carbon copy of a letter from the by now familiar folder and read: "'I have tried to respond to your question as simply as I could. Here is my answer. Scientific research is based on the idea that laws of nature determine everything that takes place, and therefore this holds for the actions of people. For this reason, a research scientist will hardly be inclined to believe that events could be influenced by a prayer, a wish granted by a supernatural Being. However, it must be admitted that our actual knowledge of these laws is only imperfect and fragmentary, so that, actually, the belief in the existence of basic all-embracing laws in Nature also rests on a sort of faith. All the same, this faith has been largely justified so far by the success of scientific research. But, on the other hand, everyone who is seriously involved in the pursuit of science becomes convinced that a spirit is manifest in the laws of the universe—a spirit vastly superior to that of man, and that in the face of which we, with our modest powers, are humbled. In this way, the pursuit of science leads to a religious feeling of a special sort, which is indeed quite different from the religiosity of someone more naive.'" The rabbi put the letter back in the folder.

"You've given me a lot to digest," I told the rabbi as I took a sip of iced tea. "If we could I would like us to return to what Einstein meant by 'a God who reveals Himself in the orderly harmony of what exists.' What is this harmony and how can we understand it?"

Just then we heard steps creaking as someone ascended the wooden stairs of the porch. "Good afternoon Rabbi and Eden." It was the mail carrier at the door. Eden took the mail and thanked him. "Jim, see you Monday. Have a good day off tomorrow." She looked through the small collection of letters in her hands and said to the rabbi, "Asher, it looks like you have a get-well card from Nat and Sarah Dolsky." Turning to me the rabbi said, "When Nat was a kid his family owned Dolsky's Stationery Store on Nassau Street. I think that I mentioned once that was the store where Albert would buy his copies of the New Republic and the Nation. Nat and his family came from Poland before the war. Nat then went back to Europe as a serviceman in the U.S. Army during World War II. He actually helped liberate Bergen-Belsen. One of the most painful gifts I ever received was from Nat. It was a collection of photos he took of the emaciated and dead bodies there. Those photos are painful not only because of what one sees in them, but also because of the reason that he took them."

"Why did he take them?" I asked.

"Because Joseph, even then, while the crematoria were still hot, he knew that there would be people who would say the Holocaust never took place. Unfortunately, Nat, who is the sweetest of people, was a prophet when it came to this. As we have seen in recent years an entire industry of Holocaust deniers try to steal the torture, suffering, murder, and death of one-third of our people. Anti-Semitism is a cancer that has been around too long for us to hope that it will go away completely. The totally misguided 'Zionism is Racism' U.N. Resolution two years ago is just another manifestation of this disease.

"Joseph, Zionism is the national liberation movement of the Jewish people. It is nationalism for the good and for the bad; all nationalisms have that duality. Remember Albert's critique of that aspect of Zionism.

"But I see something more worrisome here as well. The longer Israel holds on to the West Bank and Gaza, the intention of that occupation, no matter how benign in original intent, can only worsen. We will then see the dehumanizing aspects of that reality become the source in how both sides will act towards the other. I, too, feel a close connection to those lands, in many ways the heart of Biblical Israel, but mark my words, Israel will be forced to and will also choose to do things that will make it very easy for people to say, 'Look at those Jews, they really aren't so nice.' That in turn will allow some of the guilt that the world feels about the Holocaust to mitigate and the focus on Israel's blemishes will increase. At the same time violence done against Israel will be explained away, or even worse supported and celebrated."

"So, Rabbi, are you not a Zionist?"

"Yes, I am a Zionist, Joseph, and like Albert, I see it as the best hope for our people, even with my reservations. One of the many tragedies is that the Arab world, in part because of who the early Zionist movement aligned itself with, particularly the British during and after World War I, Zionism was perceived as an outside imperialist force, while the Zionists understood their endeavor as a long overdue homecoming. It's one of the many ill-fated misunder-

136

standings of this story.

"Joseph, I would like to go across the street to the park. The doctors say that I should take short walks. So let's take a little shpatzir."

The rabbi held my arm, and we walked across the street to a small park with a table, a bench, and a small merry-go-round on which children were whirling, giddy with delight.

"We have an interesting tradition from a time when more of us lived in small villages." the rabbi said when we were seated on the bench. "If a funeral procession and a wedding procession meet at an intersection, which one goes first?"

"I don't know."

"The wedding. Despite tragedy, despite persecution, despite death, we fill our lives with joy, freedom, and life. It was Elie Wiesel who once noted that the most amazing thing after the Holocaust was that Jews immediately started having babies, Jewish babies! Despite all that they had been through. One of the reasons I love to doven Mincha, to pray the afternoon service, is that it begins with Ashrey: 'Happy are they who dwell within Your house, may they continue to give praise to You.' The Ashrey reminds us in the middle of the day—no matter what kind of a day we are having—of the need for happiness.

"Joseph, let me return to your question about Albert's understanding of 'a God who reveals Himself in the orderly harmony of what exists.'" The rabbi paused to watch a black squirrel shoot up a tree and sit on a high branch chattering in a high pitch, its tail flicking from side to side. "Have you read the Book of Job?" he asked.

"Years ago."

"Then I must refresh your memory. For you just asked the same question that was asked of Job by the whirlwind:

"Albert's reply to such a question, yours or mine or the whirlwind's, would have been the following terse statement, 'God is sophisticated, but God is not malicious.'"

I was still not sure what he meant, so I asked the rabbi to elaborate. Eden came across the street and joined us, carrying a shawl, which she wrapped around the rabbi's shoulders.

"Thank you, my dear," he said. She sat down next to him, and he took her hand.

"Remember," said the rabbi. "Albert saw a deep connection between science and religion. As he said to me one fall afternoon, as we sat on the front porch watching the wind strip the leaves from the trees: 'If there is something in me which can be called religious, then it is the unbounded admiration for the structure of the world so far as our science can reveal it. You see, complex though the laws of nature might be, difficult though they are to understand, they are understandable by human reason, through science. God might pose difficult problems, but God never broke the rules by unanswerable ones.'"

"I heard a quote of Einstein's having to do with God and dice," I said. "Does that come into play here?"

"Very much so," replied the rabbi. "Of course, you are referring to his statement 'God does not play dice.' What does that mean? Albert believed that there was a harmonious origin, order, and design to the universe. For Albert, the throw of the dice represented chance. In Albert's mind, God would never leave things to chance. Therefore, God would not 'play dice' with the universe."

Eden added, "Albert's one-time scientific collaborator and assistant Banesh Hoffman once explained that Einstein instinctively disliked the idea of a probabilistic universe in which fundamental laws depend on chance. When facing deep problems of science, it was Albert's custom to regard things from the point of view of God.

That is why it was natural for him to seek out Asher."

"I was, of course, honored," said the rabbi. "Albert often said that God would not create a probabilistic universe," he added, taking up Eden's point. "If God was capable of creating a universe in which scientists could discern scientific laws, then God was capable of creating a universe wholly governed by such laws. He would not have created a universe in which God had to make chance decisions at every moment regarding the behavior of every individual particle."

"Did most scientists agree with him on this point?" I asked.

"No," said the rabbi. "Because of this statement, and as he grew older, he found himself removed from many in the scientific world. While the majority of the scientific community embraced quantum physics and the apparent uncertainty of subatomic particles, as Werner Heisenberg taught, Einstein was searching for a way to understand the universe that went beyond the apparent fickleness of Heisenberg's theories. He reasoned that there must be a physics beyond the unpredictability of quantum physics, and this he expounded in his Unified Field Theory."

The rabbi suggested we go back to the house for some more iced tea. As we crossed the street, he said: "Joseph, allow me to give you another teaching."

"Gladly," I said.

"What is the most famous miracle, the most famous supernatural event in the Torah?"

"The parting of the Red Sea."

"Correct. Although it is actually called the Yam Soof, the Sea of Reeds. We all grow up learning about this miracle. Yet we find a very interesting commentary in the Zohar which says that when God created the world, God also created an angel to take care of the Sea of Reeds." We entered the house and sat down at the dining room table. "One of the angel's jobs was to part the Sea of Reeds when the Israelites came to its shores. This is a fascinating notion. It is saying that this supernatural act was actually a natural act, programmed at the very beginning of time, just as a tooth is programmed to start growing when a child reaches a certain age." The rabbi paused to let me digest this and then continued. "This is not the only example we find where the rabbis tried to understand supernatural events as natural events. The Mishna contains a list of ten things that were created on the eve of the first Shabbat at twilight, right before the first week of Creation was about to come to an end. These, too, were programmed to appear at specific times, like Balaam's speaking donkey, the hole that swallowed Korach and his followers, the manna that fell in the desert, and the rainbow that appeared to Noah and his family. All of these are examples of the rabbis having a problem with a God who can break God's own rules. It was not comforting to them, nor was it to Albert.

"There is a huge gap for so many people between the theology that they are taught, or feel that they are supposed to believe, and the reality of their lives. I will never forget this little quip Albert once shared with me. It was actually on the day when I visited him at his home and that group of scientists from the Soviet Union was waiting to speak with him. 'It seems hard to sneak a look at God's cards,' Albert said, 'but that He uses 'telepathic' methods, as the present quantum theory requires of Him, is something that I cannot believe for a single moment.'"

"I know about that day!" I exclaimed, and I told the rabbi about our family's encounter with the shames in Leningrad.

"So that's how you first heard about me," the rabbi said. "You had to go all the way to Leningrad. It always amazes me how our lives turn on seemingly chance meetings, small encounters."

"Isn't that what you were saying? For God to reveal Himself, in what Einstein called, 'the orderly harmony of what exists,' there needs to be consistency in the behavior of nature." Eden smiled at the enthusiasm with which I said this.

"Bravo, Joseph," said the rabbi, "For Albert, God left clues—therefore his statement 'God is subtle, not malicious.' As Albert often exclaimed when he noted a satisfactory feature in a theory, 'This is so simple, God could not have passed it up.' On the other hand, when a new theory appeared to him that sounded arbitrary or forced, he remarked, 'God doesn't do anything like that.' For Albert, God stood for the rational connections, the laws, governing the behavior of the universe. In a moment of frustration, he once remarked to me, 'I'm not a family man. I want my peace. I want to know how God created this world. I am not interested in this or that phenomenon, in the spectrum of this or that detail. I want to know God's thoughts, the rest are details.'"

This struck me as a bit jarring. "Yes," said the rabbi, attuned to my feelings. "As we discussed once before, Albert did not hold the best view towards marriage."

I didn't enjoy contemplating this part of Einstein's life, so I changed the subject. "I once read that Einstein believed in three stages of religion," I said.

"Yes," said the rabbi. "The earliest stage was the religion of fear, followed by a religion of morality with a 'social or moral conception of God.' The rabbi read from the folder, as he tried to make sure the other pieces of paper did not fall out, quoting Einstein: "'The Jewish scriptures admirably illustrate the development from the religion of fear to moral religion ... the development from a religion of fear to moral religion is a great step in a nation's life.'" The rabbi looked up at me. "Listen closely," he said, "this is very important. 'But there is a third stage of religious experience which belongs to all of them, even though it is rarely found in pure form, and which

I will call cosmic religious feeling. It is very difficult to explain this feeling to anyone who is entirely without it, especially as there is no anthropomorphic conception of God corresponding to it. The individual feels the nothingness of human desires and aims, and the sublimity and marvelous order, which reveal themselves both in Nature and in the world of thought. He looks upon individual existence as a sort of prison and wants to experience the universe as a significant whole. The beginnings of cosmic religious feeling already appear in earlier stages of development, that is, in many of the Psalms of David and in some of the Prophets. In my view, it is the most important function of art and science to awaken this feeling and keep it alive in those who are capable of it.'" The rabbi stopped reading and looked at me.

"So you see, my young friend, Albert was a believer in a cosmic religious feeling, which he first derived from Jewish writings and then from science. The first time that he publicly talked about this 'cosmic religious feeling' was in an article in the Sunday New York Times in, I believe, November of 1930. The article generated a lot of attention. I remember Rabbi Mordechai Kaplan commented to me that he gave a sermon about a month after the article appeared called 'Why Religion is Necessary' that was a reaction to the article.

"He wrote me a short note that I have kept clipped to the article. Let me read it to you: 'The success of that sermon was based on my having connected it with Einstein's article which appeared recently in the magazine section of the N.Y. Times on Science and Religion. I doubt whether I could have managed to discuss the conception of God from the pulpit, if it had not become the subject of controversy in the press as a result of that article. On the other hand, I suspect that there was not a single person in the audience who really got the full implications of the idea that religion is now entering upon a third stage in its development by becoming cosmic.'"

"I think Kaplan and Einstein were very close in many, though not all, of their outlooks. Clearly, however, Kaplan was a firm believer in Jewish ritual and sancta as he called it. Ritual is important, for it takes our emotions, the longings of the soul, and gives them tangible form. The giving of form to the formless aids us as we encounter specific moments in our lives. Ritual also creates and establishes moments of meeting and meaning for family, friends, and community. Our lives become paced and enhanced by such a rhythm. It's one of the reasons why Shabbat is so important. Work has become the new 'opiate of the masses' as people work longer and longer hours, and we are defined increasingly by what we do for work. Work is becoming more and more both the inconvenient and convenient reason why we spend less time with our families and doing the important things that matter in our lives. I am not against dedication to work, but Shabbat reminds us to put it in its proper perspective."

"Rabbi," I said, "We use the word cosmic all the time, but what exactly does it mean?"

"I think Albert was referring to a universal law—a grand harmonious system. And I think that he was a proponent of what I see as Natural Religion, which sees the evidence of God in how the world and universe operate. With that said, can you put what he might have been getting at into your own words?"

I thought for a long moment with my eyes closed: "To be aware, to be conscious, of the harmonious state of the world as a manifestation of God's reality," I said.

"Very nice, Joseph, very nice. So you see, my young friend, Albert was a believer in a cosmic religious feeling, which he derived from Jewish writings and from science."

"Was there a connection between this 'cosmic religious feeling' of his and his lifelong quest for a unified field theory?" I asked.

"I think so. Albert believed that from observing how the stars and the planets function we could also figure out how the inside of an atom works. Albert once said, 'I am more a philosopher than a physicist.' That cosmic feeling he spoke of once in the following fashion: 'Jewish tradition contains something which finds splendid expression in many of the Psalms, namely a sort of intoxicated joy and amazement at the beauty and grandeur of this world, of which man can form just a faint notion. This joy is the feeling from which true scientific research draws its spiritual sustenance.'

"But don't confuse that with a belief in a personal God. I felt Albert was scolding me when he said to me one morning as we sat on the front steps to his house, 'It was, of course, a lie what you read about my religious convictions, a lie which is being systematically repeated. I do not believe in a personal God and I have never denied this but have expressed it clearly. If something is in me which can be called religious then it is the unbounded admiration for the structure of the world so far as science can reveal it.'"

"So why bother with religion? Why not just be a scientist if there is no point to praying to God?"

"Joseph, as I said to you a few minutes ago, prayer is an existential state where we touch the deepest reality of our lives and reality. Let me backtrack a bit here. In our first conversation I said that for Albert religion and science went hand in hand. That is not to say, though, that they are one and the same. Two hands held together may be joined but they still maintain their distinct identities. Both science and religion are quests to understand the world more deeply, but the tools and implications of that quest are not necessarily the same. The Bible opens with God calling creation 'good.' Implied in that is a moral sensitivity to how one is to relate to the world; science is not concerned with that outlook."

"Would Einstein have said that behind 'structure' lies a

144

Designer of some intelligence?"

"Albert would say that the world, the universe, works according to a structure of natural law, and that moral law is as integral to the universe as natural law. Joseph, listen very closely to what I am going to say. For centuries we thought that time, distance, energy, or mass were the constants of the universe. Albert showed us that that was not the case but rather light was the constant and so our understanding of the universe changed. The universe did not change, our understanding of it did. Related, God has not changed but our understanding of God has changed. To compound the problem we use language and images that carry with them that older understanding."

"So why don't we change them?"

"We should, at times. But within those words and images are also archetypes that hold profound meanings and wisdom."

"But Rabbi, I still don't get why I should pray."

"Joseph, why do you keep asking me that question?"

"Because," I said as I thought for a moment, "I want to pray?"

"No, that is not the right answer. Yes I know that you want to pray, just as you need to breathe. Think harder."

I sat for a few moments. I looked at the rabbi hoping for the answer. He just looked back at me waiting for my answer. Finally he said, "Joseph, the issue for you is not that you want to pray, but that you want prayer to work for you, but you are stuck with the words of the siddur, the prayer book, and a theology that doesn't work for you. When you pray you are asking that your life be made different. And that is it; as my colleague Rabbi Yaacov Cohen teaches, you should not be the same person after you have prayed. Prayer is about stepping out of our lives and into the Universe by touching God; not a God who rewards and punishes, not a God who is a physical being, not a God who can suspend the laws of nature, not a God who controls all. God is not a noun. God is the pulsating Life Force of the Universe that operates within all reality. Prayer enables us to see our lives more clearly. With that insight the rest is up to us."

The rabbi looked at his watch. "Oy, how long I have talked. We must get ready for Havdalah soon. Would you please do me a favor and see if three stars have appeared yet?"

I went out onto the porch, looking for the appearance of three stars that would signal the end of the Sabbath. They had not yet appeared and the sky, though darkening, still held the rich red cloak of dusk. From inside the dining room I could hear the rabbi joyfully singing a melody without words. I returned to the study and noticed he had placed the copy of the Book of Psalms, the same book he had been reading when I first came to visit him, on the dining room table. He had opened it to Psalm 19. Taking the book with me, I returned to the porch for my vigil. Sitting in the old rocker by the window, illuminated by a lamp inside, I began to read:

> *The heavens declare the glory of God;*
> *And the sky shows God's handiwork.*
> *Day after day the word goes forth;*
> *Night after night the story is told.*
> *Soundless the speech, voiceless the talk,*
> *Yet the story is echoed throughout the world.*

I turned the pages to where a worn leather marker had been placed. It was Psalm 104:

> *Bless the Lord, my soul.*
> *O Lord, my God, You are great indeed,*
> *clothed in grandeur and glory,*
> *wrapped in light as in a garment,*
> *unfolding the heavens like a curtain.*
> *On waters You lay the beams of Your chambers;*

*You take the clouds for Your chariot,*
*riding the wings of the wind.*
*You make the winds your angels,*
*fire and flame Your servants.*
*You set the earth on its foundation*
*so that it should never collapse.*

I finished reading and once again looked up to the sky. There were still no stars, but a radiant dark deep blue was now rolling across the heavens. The rabbi came out onto the porch. "Joseph," he said. "I hope that you have noticed that Shabbat ends not by looking into a prayer book or at a watch, but rather by looking up towards the heavens. Judaism asks us to really notice the world and universe that we live in and of which we are a part. It is a lifelong process of discovery and self-discovery to reach, as Albert put it, 'that cosmic religious feeling.' I use the Bible and the Talmud and the wisdom of Jewish philosophy. Albert used physics. These two paths are the same path."

We both looked up and saw three stars in the sky. "Come inside and let us make Havdalah." I followed the rabbi into the dining room for the short ceremony that separates the Sabbath from the workweek. Eden joined us as she lit the braided Havdalah candle, its flame illuminating her face. The rabbi held a cup of wine, and I was given a silver spice box to hold. The rabbi explained, "We begin Shabbat with two separate candles and end with a braided candle symbolizing coming together and wholeness, shlemoot, the pace that Shabbat gives to our lives. The wine and spices both come from our world—the former is an example of how we alter and use the world for human benefit, while the latter is an example of how we use the world without altering it. On Shabbat, we leave the world alone: with the start of the new week we once again engage in the world, God's gift to us." After the ceremony we wished each other

147

shavuah tov, a good week to come.

"Joseph," Eden said, "thank you so much for coming. That you came home so soon just to see Asher made this a very special Shabbas for both of us." The rabbi and I walked slowly out to the porch. A gentle breeze was blowing. I shook his hand and thanked him for our conversation. He wished me luck with my exams at the end of the semester.

"Please come see me when you're home again," the rabbi said.

"Of course," I replied, my eyes shining.

As I walked toward Nassau Street with all of its Saturday night energy, lights, and noise, I thought of the Psalms and the three stars and the line "Do you know the ordinances of the heavens?" from the Book of Job. I didn't know, nor did Einstein. But the rabbi had awakened in me the conviction that the search for that answer is what gives our lives meaning. Einstein and the rabbi had shown me that it is the seeking, not the finding, that connects us to the Life Force of the Universe.

# 19

# Wrestling

When I came home from my visit with the rabbi, my parents were waiting for me.

"Joseph," my mother said before I even had the door closed,

"we would like to talk with you."

Her tone sounded portentous, and I followed them into the living room, rather than to our large eat-in kitchen where we usually talked. We sat down stiffly on the two facing sofas, me on one, they on the other.

"We don't want you to take this the wrong way," my father said. "But your mother and I are a bit concerned about all the time you're spending with the rabbi."

"We've been through this," I said. "Why are you so worried? Are you afraid I might become religious?" I felt my blood begin to boil.

"Joseph, that's not it," said my father.

"Then what is it?"

"We know that children leave home and grow up and create their own lives. We are happy that you have found a teacher." He paused and sighed. "But we don't know what he is teaching you."

"Is he one of those Lubavitch rabbis that brainwash young people?" my mother spit out, panic in her voice.

"No, he's not. And even if he is, so what? Everyone has their own path."

"There are limits," said my mother.

"Oh, so this is about limits," I shot back. "Where's the line. At keeping Shabbas? At eating Kosher? At wearing a yarmulke? At becoming a rabbi?"

"I knew it!" my mother said to my father. "He wants to become a rabbi."

"And what if I did. It's not like becoming a priest. You'll get your precious grandchildren eventually."

"Don't speak to your mother like that," my father said.

I saw them make an effort to collect themselves. "We don't want you to make a choice that you might come to regret," said my father.

"Regret?" I blurted out. "You were the ones who gave me this identity! Think about it. Wherever we traveled in Europe, we always looked for synagogues. It struck me as a bit odd, since we hardly ever went to synagogue here. That sent a clear message to me that my Jewish identity was important and mattered. Isn't that what you wanted?"

"Of course, Joseph," said my father. "We want you to be proud of your Jewish heritage, but ..."

"But what?" I exploded. "Give me a break. I remember on the first visit to Europe in 1967 we went to Florence and saw Michelangelo's David. And what did you say to me, Mom? You explained that the statue was modeled after Hercules and represented Florentine freedom and civic duty. I replied that I thought it was a statue of King David about to fight Goliath? And do you remember how you responded? You said the statue represented something much bigger than the Biblical figure of David. You said that Michelangelo had taken David from the Bible and made him represent strength and freedom in a Platonic sense. You said he was the humanistic ideal and represented the Western view of man's preeminence and beauty. But what struck me then was that you seemed so happy to see King David removed from the Bible."

"I'm stunned you remember this," said my mother. "I had no idea it was so significant to you."

"I know! You've never been able to see it. You've never understood me. Or maybe you've understood me too well, and you've wanted to temper any connection to Judaism which seemed to go beyond your sense of what it is to be a Jew!"

"What we're worried about is that you'll become religious," said my father. "And being religious, from what we've seen, means having judgments about those of us who are not religious. It means not being rational or grounded in reality."

And then it hit me. That what I had been wrestling with about science and religion, the rational and mystical, fact and faith, were not my questions about religion. They were my parents' questions, or rather my parents' outlook on the spiritual life. I was wrestling not with religion, but with my parents' view of religion. I was wrestling with my parents.

With that, I felt an enormous release of energy. It was as if I had finally broken free of their gravitational field. I was spun out, flying through space! I felt so open, flying into a vast field of consciousness, where there was an overwhelming Presence beyond who I was—beyond who I am! I felt like throwing my hands in the air and doing the same dance that I had seen the Hassidim do at the Wall. But I restrained myself. Instead, I said as gently as I could to my parents, "Please don't worry: I will always be your son." I went over to each of them and kissed them on the head. Then I went up to my room.

A few minutes later there was a knock on my door. "Joseph, we have something we feel we need to say to you now."

"Mom and Papa, let's just leave it as it is."

"No, Joseph, we insist," as they opened the door.

I sat at the end of my bed. My mother sat in a chair and my father stood next to her. "Joseph, it is time that we tell you," my mother said.

"Tell me what?"

My parents both glanced at each other and my father reached over and held both of my mother's shoulders. "Joseph the reason I was pregnant at our wedding was not because of your father."

I could not quite follow, which they could see by the expression on my face.

"Joseph, you know that Zayda was a Zionist. He like many Americans not only gave money, but also during the War of Independence helped smuggle guns to the Israeli army. Somehow he got a gun and needed to get it delivered to an Israeli agent. He did not want to go himself since he thought he was under surveillance by the police. So he asked me to deliver the gun. He told me to go to a room in a hotel in New York and deliver the gun to whoever was in the room. I delivered the gun and then." She stopped talking and tears filled her eyes and she looked down at the floor. My father started to say something, but my mother said, "It's okay, I want to tell him. The Zionist agent raped me and I soon found out that I was pregnant. Your father and I had only known each other three months at that time. I told him that I would not get an abortion and if he wanted to leave me I would understand. Instead he said he would marry me. Joseph, your father is a true—what's the word?"

"Tzadik, Mom," I said, barely able to get the words out.

"We never told anyone the truth we just told you, even our parents and our siblings, except for Nathan shortly before he got married."

"Joseph," my father then added, "we are telling you this now for two reasons. First, it was always our intent to tell you at some point, and second, so you understand part of our fear as we watch you become more Jewish. Judaism did not prevent what your great-grandfather did to your great-grandmother, and Zionism did not protect your mother."

That night the dream returned. Then the statue of David was using his sling to sling rocks at the walls of Galleria, causing the walls to crash down.

# 20

## A Blessing

The next morning I knocked on the rabbi's door. Eden opened it.

"Joseph, good morning. Is it summer already?"

"No. I'm sorry to bother you."

"I'm not sure if Asher is up. The most important thing for him now is rest."

I stood downcast, irresolute.

"What is it, my dear?" Eden asked.

"When I came home yesterday I had a fight with my parents about all the time I have been spending here."

Eden sighed. "I wondered if it might come to that. Come in. I'll check if Asher can see you."

I sat in the living room. I could hear the sound of conversation upstairs, and then heard feet descending.

"Joseph," said the rabbi as I rose. Eden followed him into the room. He looked wan and sallow, dressed in white pajamas and a robe of coarse white cotton. "Please tell me what happened." He sat down heavily in his chair. I could tell by the look on Eden's face that she would have preferred him to be in bed, and I wondered how much our conversations might be tiring him.

After I told him what had happened, but not the part about my mother, the rabbi said, "This is good." I looked at him, wanting

153

an explanation. "There is the tension of wanting to embrace all of what our parents give us, while at the same time not wanting to be smothered by it. The Amidah prayer opens by speaking about the 'God of our ancestors' as well as the 'God of Abraham, the God of Isaac, the God of Jacob.' We know in this context that ancestors refer to Abraham, Isaac, and Jacob so it could be seen as being redundant. But the Baal Shem Tov and Martin Buber teach that we are Jewish because it was handed to us by our ancestors, starting with our parents, but also because we must find our own path. There is a tension in the two, yet they are both essential. Your encounter yesterday was an important step in your own self-realization."

"But Rabbi, there is more that happened yesterday." I then told him what my parents had told me.

"Joseph, I am very sorry to hear that. There is no ...."

Before he could go on I said, "But Rabbi, why bother with all of this?"

"Joseph, if you are looking for perfection in this world then you will be a very disappointed person. The moment we were given free choice, or rather the moment we realized that we had free choice in the Garden of Eden, perfection went out the window. This is part of our challenge to create a world with the peace of the Garden before we ate from the fruit, but with the knowledge we gained after we ate from it. That is part of what it means to be a human being. If you will, the social being that we are is how we interact with the world we live in. But there is another aspect: the internal self, our soul work. It is just as important as our external work."

"But now what do I do?"

"Be yourself! There will be other discoveries and events along the way. Every neshama, every soul, has its own path to fulfill, a soul quest. During the Second World War there were Jewish children that were given over to monasteries for safekeeping. When the war was over, the Zionist movement sent representatives to find these children. Records had not been well kept at one of these monasteries, so no one knew who the Jewish children were. The representatives spent the day there, but to no avail. As they were getting ready to leave, all the children were brought out to the lawn. One of the representatives called out, 'Sh'ma Yisreal Adonai Eloheynu, Adonai Ehad.' Suddenly, seven of the children called out, "Mama, Papa." The last thing that these children had heard every night when their parents put them to bed was the Sh'ma. Through all those years of darkness and separation their souls never forgot who they were. Joseph, you no longer have to fight who you really are, who you want to be. Listen to that still small voice that echoes in your heart, that reflects the timeless echo of the universe. Feed it, and let it grow."

I was deeply moved, unable to speak.

"Now," said the rabbi, "Joseph, lean close to me." The rabbi placed his hands on my head, intoning, "'May you experience enjoyment of the good things in this world, and for worlds still to come; may you trust in generations past and yet to be; may your heart meditate with understanding, and your mouth speak wisdom, and your tongue be moved to song; let your eyes look forward, your gaze be straight ahead enlightened by the light of the Torah and your face be radiant as the brightness of the firmament; may your lips utter knowledge and may your heart rejoice in righteousness and your steps hurry to hear the words of the Ancient of Days.'

"One day you will know that passage from the Talmud, Joseph, and, one day, God willing, you, too, will bless your children with it."

The rabbi lifted his hands from my head and I looked towards him. "There is one more thing, Joseph. When I die, will you please say kaddish for me?"

I nodded, unable to speak.

"As you have probably guessed," the rabbi said, "Eden and I don't have any children."

"But Rabbi, you're not dying, are you?" I finally managed to say.

The rabbi laughed. "Not yet, I hope."

Eden came in. "Asher, I must insist. Now it's time to rest."

With deep gratitude in my heart, I rose to leave. The rabbi whispered something to Eden.

"Wait a little, Joseph," he said. "I have something for you."

Eden left the room and came back with a book and a pen. The rabbi opened the book and wrote something in it. He handed it to me and said, "Joseph, you have dreamed the dream. You have been at the Temple. I once said I would tell you about the goat in your dream." He paused for a moment and then continued. "From talking to you over the past months, it's clear to me that goat represents your life as service to God. As you will learn, that path is about sacrifice, service, and offering. It's important that you understand the meaning of sacrifice, for it is in the sacrificial act that we reveal our humanity. One of the words for sacrifice is korban, related to keruv: to bring close. The path you are on will bring you and the people you will touch with your words and your derekh eretz, the path of your life, closer to God. Become who you are meant to be. Carve and shape your life, always listening to the hopes and passions of your heart. Let your neshama, your soul, sing."

I looked at the book and recognized it as the Book of Psalms that he had given to Einstein; the book he had been reading when I first met him. I opened it. There was an inscription at the top of the title page:

*To Albert,*

*"The basic principle of all basic principles and the pillar of all sciences is to realize that there is a First Being who brought every existing thing into being. All existing things, whether celestial, terrestrial, or belonging to an intermediate class, exist only through His true existence." — Maimonides*

> *Shalom,*
> *Asher*
> *Princeton, N.J.*
> *December 3, 1936/19 Kislev, 5697*

At the bottom of the page he had written:

*To Joseph,*
*"Behold, the dreamer comes." — Genesis 37:19*

> *Shalom and love,*
> *Asher*
> *Princeton, N.J.*
> *May 15,1977/27 Iyar, 5737*

# Coda

It was 4 a.m. and my travel alarm clock had just gone off. The smooth-sounding hip-hop song "Where Is The Love" by the Black Eyed Peas was playing on the station I had set the clock. The song first reached the charts in June of 2003 and remained near the top of the charts all summer long leading up to the second anniversary of September 11th. Like an anthem the song would not go away, reflecting the questions still left unanswered by September 11th and the ensuing events that had followed in the interim two years.

*Yo, whatever happened to the values of humanity*
*Whatever happened to the fairness in equality*
*Instead in spreading love we spreading animosity*
*Lack of understanding, leading lives away from unity*
*That's the reason why sometimes I'm feelin' under*
*That's the reason why sometimes I'm feelin' down*
*There's no wonder why sometimes I'm feelin' under*
*Gotta keep my faith alive to lovers bound*
*People killin', people dyin'*
*Children hurt and you hear them cryin'*
*Can you practice what you preach*
*And would you turn the other cheek*
*Father, Father, Father help us*
*Send us some guidance from above*
*'Cause people got me, got me questionin'*
*Where is the love*

I was in New York again to help the Red Cross during the official memorial service. We were to report at 5 a.m. next to Ground Zero. As I made my way to the meeting spot at the corner of Chambers Street and West Broadway, I found myself at the corner where I had first seen the wounded towers two years earlier. There was something strangely peaceful and serene at that hour; a full moon was in the late-night sky where the North Tower had stood.

I was struck by the local specific intensity of the day. In the lower level of Ground Zero families gathered to remember and mourn, and near the edge of the upper perimeter children read each of the names of those who had perished, ending with their father or mother or a close relative. Just beyond the podium there was a fence that circled that gaping hole. There the public could try to get a peek of what was going on inside. Further out on the west and east sides of the site traffic flowed on West Street and Broadway. Even during the four separate moments of silence—at the time when each tower was hit and fell—the traffic continued. I thought of Israel, where when national moments of silence fall the entire country comes to a standstill. Here the width of a curbstone and life carried on as though nothing important was happening.

Around the entire perimeter fence someone had taped the message "AMPLIFY LOVE, DISSIPATE HATE." Near the end of the afternoon as I made way towards Broadway I noticed that someone had tied to the perimeter fence a bed sheet. On the sheet they had written in magic marker:

*The abolition of war will demand distasteful limitations of national sovereignty. But what perhaps impedes understanding of the situation more than anything else is that the term "mankind" feels vague and abstract. People scarcely realize in imagination that the danger is to themselves and their children and their grandchildren, and not only to a dimly apprehended humanity. They can scarcely bring themselves to grasp that they, individually, and those whom they love are in imminent danger of perishing agonizingly. And so they hope that perhaps war may be allowed to continue provided modern weapons are prohibited.*

*This hope is illusory.*

*There lies before us, if we choose, continual progress in happiness, knowledge, and wisdom. Shall we, instead, choose death, because we cannot forget our quarrels? We appeal as human beings to human beings: Remember your humanity, and forget the rest. If you can do so, the way lies open to a new Paradise; if you cannot, there lies before you the risk of universal death.*

*Russell-Einstein Manifesto*
*July 9, 1955*

I read its words and took some solace that the world was still here almost fifty years after they had been written, but also realized that the world had entered a new chapter two years earlier. Now the questions posed in the Manifesto were even more acute.

A group of people, on their own and not part of the official ceremony, had gathered not too far from the sheet. They were taking turns reading out loud from the New York Times book Portraits of Grief. The collection of short essay sketches about those who had been killed on September 11th that had run every day for months after the attacks. A semicircle formed out from the fence along Broadway under the strong afternoon sun.

As I stood there I became aware of a couple standing behind me with a young child in a stroller. The mother then said, "Adam, I think Hope wants some Cheerios." I turned around briefly and saw the woman who I had helped get a taxi two years earlier. She and her husband had named their daughter Hope.

**Author's note:**

Einstein's Rabbi reads like non-fiction but is a work of fiction. It has that feel because all direct quotes attributed to Einstein that the reader will find in this novella were actually said or written by him at some time during his life. In addition, all the references to biographical data about Einstein are historically accurate, with the exception of any interaction with Einstein's rabbi, which is entirely fictitious.

Michael M. Cohen

**About the Author:**

Michael Margaretten Cohen was born in Bloomington, Indiana and raised in Ewing, New Jersey. He graduated from the University of Vermont in History with Honors. He received ordination from the Reconstructionist Rabbinical College and served as the Rabbi of the Israel Congregation in Manchester Center, Vermont for ten years. During that time he also served as the President of the Reconstructionist Rabbinical Association. Rabbi Cohen was a founding faculty member of The Arava Institute for Environmental Studies (www.arava.org) located on Kibbutz Ketura in 1996 while on sabbatical from the Israel Congregation. The Arava Institute is the premier environmental teaching and research program in the Middle East preparing future Arab and Jewish leaders to cooperatively solve the regions environmental challenges. Presently he is the Director of Special Projects for the Arava Institute dividing his time with his family between Manchester Center, Vermont and Kibbutz Ketura, Israel. He is the author of numerous articles that have appeared in the United States and the Middle East. He sits on the Board of Burr & Burton Academy, as well as the Tree and Energy Committees of the Town of Manchester Center. *Einstein's Rabbi* is his first published book.

The author is grateful for permission to include the following previously copyrighted material: